A
CENTER
OF
QUIET

HEARING GOD WHEN
LIFE IS NOISY

David Runcorn

INTERVARSITY PRESS
DOWNERS GROVE, ILLINOIS 60515

InterVarsity Press
P.O. Box 1400, Downers Grove, Illinois 60515, U.S.A.

© *1990 David Runcorn*

Published in the United States of America by InterVarsity Press, Downers Grove, Illinois, with permission from Darton, Longman & Todd Ltd., London, England. Originally published in England in the Daybreak edition as Space for God.

InterVarsity Press is the book-publishing division of InterVarsity Christian Fellowship, a student movement active on campus at hundreds of universities, colleges and schools of nursing in the United States of America, and a member movement of the International Fellowship of Evangelical Students. For information about local and regional activities, write Public Relations Dept., InterVarsity Christian Fellowship, 6400 Schroeder Rd., P.O. Box 7895, Madison, WI 53707-7895.

All Scripture quotations, unless otherwise indicated, are from the Holy Bible, New International Version. Copyright © *1973, 1978, International Bible Society. Used by permission of Zondervan Bible Publishers.*

ISBN 0-8308-1739-5

Printed in the United States of America

Library of Congress Cataloging-in-Publication Data

Runcorn, David.
   A center of quiet: hearing God when life is noisy/by
David Runcorn.
      p.   cm.
   Includes bibliographical references.
   ISBN 0-8308-1739-5
   1. Silence—Religious aspects—Christianity.   2. Solitude—
Religious aspects—Christianity.   3. Spiritual life.   I. Title.
BV4509.5.R86   1990
248.4'7—dc20   90-49047
                                                            CIP

13	12	11	10	9	8	7	6	5	4	3	2	1
99	98	97	96	95	94	93	92	91	90			

To the villagers of
Embd,
near Zermatt, Switzerland,
who, in Summer 1987,
shared the silence of their mountain
and sheltered an amateur hermit

FOREWORD

In these days when there is such an abundance of books on spirituality, one might be tempted to wonder, 'Why another?', especially as so much has been said down through the ages about the need for space and silence before God. But, if yet more is being said, it is because the need is all the greater today. We need that constant recall to a life that is continually being nourished by the creative power in solitude and silence, and that recall has to be expressed in fresh, contemporary terms against the background of present day society.

It is both exciting and encouraging to read of another's spiritual journey and to recognise the familiar paths and landmarks. It is rather like looking at someone's holiday photos which fascinate us if we have visited the same place and whet our appetites if we haven't.

In *A Center of Quiet,* David Runcorn does this. He both takes us back to familiar places in our prayer journey and also beckons us to explore with him new ones . . . and he does so in a delightfully refreshing and easy style that makes the book extremely readable. Although this is by no means a spiritual autobiography, it is very helpfully illustrated from the author's personal experience and this ensures that the reflections are 'earthed'.

Over the years that I have known him – at theological college, as Chaplain of the Lee Abbey Fellowship, and as a priest – I have increasingly come to appreciate David's poetic touch, in his preaching, his writing and indeed in his superb photography. And this touch results in some absolute gems here in *A Center of Quiet*. They sparkle like dewdrops glistening on grass in the early morning light. This is a gentle, almost whimsical, sharing of insights that have been gleaned over years of faithful pursuit of the contemplative way, and the book is rich in quotations from a wide range of spiritual writers.

All that he claims about silence and space is authenticated by his own experience of them which he shares very frankly – from parish life, community life and more recently from his period of hermit life in an Alpine cabin. There kneeling on the bare boards, often with tears as his only language of prayer, he explored the inner reality of space for God. In that environment he discovered the cost and the reward of silence before the living God. The glimpses David gives of this time are very moving. But if we find ourselves longing rather wistfully for a similar opportunity (in an equally beautiful setting) we are left in no doubt about the qualities of spiritual toughness, inner strength, balance and discipline needed to cope with any prolonged solitude.

There is much wisdom in this book and it repays careful reading (even though it is tempting to romp through it, so interesting is its content and attractive its style). Each chapter ends with further thoughts for reflection and suggestions for practical follow up which will be useful both to individuals and to prayer groups.

Here is a book written by one who has been courageous in his own exploration of prayer. It will encourage those who are weary or disheartened and refresh those for whom the wells are beginning to run dry. I cannot imagine that anyone will read it without finding their love-longing for God intensifying and the desire to give him more space in their lives deepening.

SISTER MARGARET MAGDALEN CSMV
St Mary's Convent
Wantage, Oxon.

INTRODUCTION

A book devoted to discussing silence is something of a contradiction and should be treated with great suspicion! Books also have a way of invading spaces for God and filling them with second-hand ideas. Let's be honest, one of the surest ways to avoid silence and solitude is to read a book about it. But, having started with such a confession, I must try and describe the purpose of this book.

In ancient times, in little known or hazardous parts of a country there was a practice of marking a trail by 'cairns'. In the Lake District they were often small piles of stones. In the marshlands of East Anglia it is said that St Boniface marked the safe ways with wooden posts. They were not the only routes, but for fellow travellers they were marker guides to paths that had proved safe and trust-worthy.[1] Through the deserts and mountains of the Bible this was often done. Sometimes they marked a simple way through the wilderness. At other times such cairns marked the progress of journeys of far deeper significance. They marked places of discovery, of revelation and covenant and commitment. They marked out meeting places between heaven and earth – meetings with the living God. And their names preserved for ever the memory of those encounters. So it was that Jacob set up a cairn altar in the wilderness, marking the place where the ladder from heaven had touched the earth and God had spoken to him. For 'surely the Lord is in this place, and I was not aware of it . . . This is none other than the house of God' (Gen. 28:16–17). And so he called the placed Bethel – house of God.

This is a book of cairns, of marker-posts and 'altars'. It is not a blueprint, but a collection of fragments, reflections, experiences and journeys gathered around the themes of silence, solitude and the Christian life. It is intended to be more of a workbook, or perhaps even a scrapbook – a companion for fellow travellers. It is written for those who are willing to practise solitude and silence, and to explore it for themselves in their own lives. It is my hope that this book can in some measure be 'lived' rather than thought about and discussed; we are far too full of *ideas* already.

The first section, 'The Call to Solitude', explores the whole experience of solitude and being alone – both in our own lives and in the life of Jesus. The second section, 'The Companionship of Silence', looks at the biblical understanding of silence through an extended reflection on the place of the desert in the Scriptures. The final section, 'In the Midst of Life', reflects on the importance of silence in shaping Christian prayer and of our awareness of the presence of God in the world.

A Center of Quiet is written to be taken in little bits at a time, perhaps by individuals or by groups. It is not a book to be hurried. The end of each chapter offers suggestions for practical reflection, activity and prayer. But these are only starting points for the reader to take the themes further. Above all, it is a book that seeks to *leave* spaces for God, not to *fill* them.

Cairns can only mark the wanderings of a fellow traveller. Though we often find ourselves travelling together (in the fellowship we call the church), the path for each of us is uniquely our own. And it is Christ who must lead us.

DAVID RUNCORN

PART I

THE CALL TO SOLITUDE

ONE

GETTING ALONE

Very early in the morning, while it was still dark, Jesus got up, left the house, and went off to a solitary place, where he prayed.

Mark 1:35

Can you imagine what that 'solitary place' was like? It always feels bleak and a bit haunted to me. It can also mean 'lonely', 'desolate' or 'wild'. The disciples woke to find him missing and went out to look for him. There, in a 'solitary place', a long way from anywhere or anyone, they found him, wrapped up against the chill of the dawn. He was praying.

What did they feel when they finally stumbled upon him? Relief at finding him? Perhaps they also felt awkward. It is always rather embarrassing to burst in on something so private as prayer. But this Jesus was such a contrast to the man of authority and supernatural power among the crowds in Nazareth the day before. What was he doing here of all places? He was a man for the world – what was he doing in the wilderness?

How often they must have felt out of their depth with Jesus. He lived with such a different set of priorities. They could never be sure what he was going to do next, who he might talk to, where the road would take them. Jesus disturbed them as much as he comforted them. The disciples followed him around in a haze of loving confusion, knowing only that when he spoke and acted, it was like a glimpse of another world among them.

And now, breathless and sweaty, they have stumbled into this place of absolute stillness. What a shock! Perhaps this was their first glimpse into the secret heart of the life of Jesus. Had they known better, they might have realised that they too should sit quietly. But most of us feel an uneasy mixture of attraction and dread in the presence of true silence. On that morning it was too much for them. They broke into the silence: 'Everyone is looking for you!'

A pattern of silence

In the weeks and months that followed, his disciples discovered that this regular withdrawal from people and activity was the one predictable thing about Jesus. He made silence and solitude his special companions. Whatever the demands upon him, he always found a time and place to hide away and be alone. His hectic teaching and ministering was constantly punctuated by these times of withdrawal. Before all the most important events in his life we find him preparing by getting alone. His ministry began in the wilderness (Matt. 4:1–11). He chose his disciples after a whole night alone in prayer (Luke 6:12). When John the Baptist died Jesus spent time alone (Matt. 14:13). Before the glory of the transfiguration and darkness of the cross we find him alone in prayer (Matt. 17:1–9 and 26:36–46). In those lonely places the deep springs of the Spirit's life renewed him, the Father's will strengthened him and the Father's love inspired him.

He taught the disciples to do the same. After one particularly busy time of ministry and teaching he said, ' "Come with me by yourselves to a quiet place and get some rest." So they went away by themselves in a boat to a lonely place' (Mark 6:31–2).

This was the secret of Jesus' life. This was where he found strength to follow the Father's will. When we follow him we must copy not only his words and actions but his silence and moments of solitary withdrawing as well. If Jesus needed those times, then we certainly need them more! Like the disciples we follow him into the desert places. And in our turn, we must learn from him how to be alone and still.

The commas and full stops of silence

If you have a magazine or newspaper handy, try reading any article without using the punctuation marks. It doesn't make much sense does it? It all becomes a hectic string of words. The meaning is lost. It lacks direction. The purpose of punctuation in a piece of writing is to guide the reader into the true meaning of the words and phrases; through it we understand. Punctuation also gives life and purpose to the words. Next time you see your favourite actor or actress on television, notice how cleverly they use timing – pauses and spaces – to give the words their meaning and power.

Punctuation is a helpful way of thinking about Jesus' relationship with silence and solitude. Jesus punctuated his life with silence and solitude. His times alone were the commas, pauses and full stops in the story of his life. They gave the rest of his life its structure, direction and balance. His words and his works were born out of those hours of silent waiting upon God.

Silence is for everyone

Jesus didn't love silence because he was a 'quiet type' or a mystic. It wasn't just a matter of temperament. The Hollywood films of Jesus always imply this – blond hair, brilliant blue eyes and a mind always half elsewhere. He is always 'the quiet, sensitive reflective type' (with occasional outbursts!).

Jesus' need and love for solitude was something deeper than temperament. He certainly had a quiet, reflective side to him, but he also had a lively and even aggressive side. He loved being alone, but was also accused of enjoying parties too much! If he sometimes spoke like a mystic, about another world that was coming, there was also no one more down to earth in the way he spoke and lived.

Clearly his times alone in prayer were not to satisfy a part of his character – he came to solitude with his whole being. He needed solitude first of all because he was a human being. For Jesus, solitude was the place in which all the rich diversity of his temperament, personality and humanity were drawn together and offered to the Father.

This is important, because we can too easily assume that solitude is only for certain types of people. It is true that people will differ in how easily they respond to it, but the solitude that Jesus urges us to seek is for all of us. It is a much deeper matter than temperamental preferences. After all, when we speak of someone's temperament we are usually summing up a person's character by their dominant characteristic – the way they offer themselves to the world around. In that way we describe someone as 'extrovert', 'introvert', 'thoughtful', or 'outgoing', for example. That is not wrong. But at best it is only a starting point. At worst it becomes a superficial label.

Solitude is the place where the whole of our personality and being, seen and unseen, is drawn together in the transforming presence of God's love. But more than that, the silence of solitude is the silence of eternity. We are drawn into the mystery of something much bigger than ourselves. It places us, with all that he has made, in the heart of God's cosmic love and presence. It is there that life is renewed, restored and given its true perspective.

Finding a place

When Jesus taught the disciples to pray he was very practical. 'When you pray, go into your room, close the door and pray to your Father, who is unseen. Then your Father, who sees what is done in secret, will reward you.' (Matt. 6:6). His teaching is fascinating here. He is saying, 'as God is unseen, you must be unseen if you wish to find him. Go into a secret place by yourself and there you will find the One who wants to share your secret and bless you for it. So find somewhere where you can close the door and be alone.'

While visiting Israel a few years ago I was shown archaeological remains of typical houses from the time of Jesus and before. They were mostly open plan. Only the very wealthy had private rooms with doors. Jesus himself had to leave the house in order to get alone. Clearly our modern homes give us far more opportunity to 'close the door' than most of Jesus' audience would have had. So 'closing the door' must be more deeply a call to an inner withdrawing. 'Closing the door' is learning to keep a solitary secret place at the centre of our lives. Outer solitude is in order to learn inner solitude. Russian Orthodox Christians call this place a *poustinia* – a little desert in the heart.[1] In our *poustinia* all the diverse and fragmented activities that make up our lives can be brought into the silence of God's presence, there to be loved and integrated and renewed with deeper purpose.

But most of us need an actual place to begin. Geography is important. It may be a room, or the corner of a room. Perhaps it is a particular chair. If your own home is too noisy there may be a friend who has a room you can 'borrow' for an hour or so. In one crowded student digs my 'lonely place' was the bathroom, before anyone else was up!

Whatever we choose, it needs to be a regular commitment – not a place to visit only as the mood takes us. Decide how long you are going to be still. Once there, keep the time simple and don't be tempted to fill it up with prayers or reading. Give the time to God and be still. There are some suggestions for using such time at the end of this chapter.

Finding the time

Life is very pressured for some people. For very practical reasons it is not always easy to make a lot of time for praying. If you are a parent with young children, for example, there are times when it is just not possible! This book does not assume that the reader has lots of time. There may be only a few minutes a day for some people. But there are ways of using just a few minutes. It is quality not quantity that matters. Why should long prayer times be any more 'meaningful' than short ones? Jesus himself warned against praying prayers that were too long. (Matt. 6:7). God can use the few moments of space that are offered to him in the middle of a hectic day. It may be stopping for a moment by the sink (some people keep prayer cards or pictures above the kitchen sink for such a purpose). It may be closing your eyes in the corner of a commuter train or at the desk at work. Some of the ideas in this book help us to offer our *moments* and our days as space for God.

Quiet time and unquiet time

Soon after Christianity became more real for me, I began studying at a Bible College. I will never forget the experience of being regularly woken up, early in the morning, by the noise of loud singing to the beat of a very large tambourine. In the room below mine a Scottish Pentecostal student called Ian was having his 'Quiet Time'. In the course of a week he sang his way through most of *Redemption Hymnal*, and if he ran out of hymns he just made up a few more as he went along!

9

I was relatively new to the evangelical style of worship and prayer at the time, and this traumatic (if challenging) awakening at the start of each day made a lasting impression on me. The 'Quiet Time', I quickly discovered, was what evangelical Christians called the discipline of daily prayer and Bible-reading. To guide the time there were plenty of aids such as Bible-reading notes and even handy memory devices to give structure to the praying (such as ACTS – Adoration, Confession, Thanksgiving, Supplication).

In such a way, my own praying and Bible-reading at last found some sort of discipline and structure. I was grateful for it. But I could never understand why it was called 'Quiet Time'. In my experience it wasn't. It was all very busy and full of activity. At the very least it had to include a Bible reading and study, self-examination and confession, thanksgiving, praise and the intercession list. It was more like a spiritual business meeting (and there is a place for that). But wasn't there supposed to be quietness somewhere in it? Where was the time to learn to be silent, to set aside all the activity and concerns and be open to God?

I had a suspicion that it wasn't only my problem. Even the College Quiet Day once a term was not noticeably any quieter. Instead of a day full of academic lectures it was full of devotional talks. It wasn't really quiet – just a different sort of noise. Though we were all exhorting each other to be quiet before God, we were actually succeeding in avoiding this. We needed to be honest and fact the fact that we were running away from silence. For all the many valuable things we were learning together at college, we had not yet learned to follow Jesus into the desert to pray.

It was through meeting Christians from the Catholic and Orthodox traditions of the Church that I at last began to follow Jesus into the desert and learn to be alone and silent before God. More recently I had the opportunity to spend a summer alone in a small cabin high up in the Swiss Alps. Before I went I sought the advice of a friend, a Franciscan monk. I told him all the books I was planning to take with me. 'I want to really *use* the time up there,' I said, sounding braver than I felt! His reply was very firm. 'You've got far too much theology in your head already. Just take your Bible and read a verse a day. That's all you need.' He was right. Even in planning time alone I was trying to avoid being alone.

For reflection

Think of some of the moments and places where you could be quiet during the day.

Take a sheet of paper and chart your week's activities. Where are the punctuation marks? Have you got full stops and pauses and commas that balance out all the activities? Are there enough of them?

What is your experience of being quiet and alone with God? What attracts you to, and what makes you uneasy with, the ideas of getting alone?

Begin by choosing a comfortable but alert posture. An upright chair is quite good. If you are kneeling, have you tried a prayer stool? It enables you to sit back on your heels without causing your legs to go numb or painful.[2]

Sit quietly for a moment, letting your body settle down. Let your breathing find its rhythm. Deepen your breathing slightly (when we are busy our breathing is often shallow). Let your body relax into this rhythm for a while.

Breathe in with the prayer 'Lord Jesus Christ'. Welcome Christ into the depths of your being like the fresh air that is filling your lungs. As you breathe out, silently pray, 'Have mercy on me.' Invite Christ to clear out the clutter and noise within, creating a *poustinia*, an inner room, where you can meet the Father in secret. Quietly repeat this prayer for a while on the rhythm of your breathing. When you are ready, be completely silent for a moment and then, if you wish to, close with a prayer of your own, offering to God the concerns and longings that are part of your life at present.

You might consider using this way of praying for a few minutes before and after reading a section of this book. Try to make it a regular punctuation – it doesn't need to be more more than a few minutes. And part of the gift of this prayer is that it can be used anywhere and at any time. Let it punctuate your day. You can pray this way while jammed in a commuter train, going round the supermarket or (from personal experience) while operating a noisy commercial dishwasher!

TWO

WITH MY WHOLE SELF

If a man is to turn his heart towards God, he must first of all *return* to his heart, from which he is so often absent.

Sister John Oxenham

. . . what we will be has not yet been made known. But we know that when he appears, we shall be like him.

John 3:2

'YOU ARE HERE!' said the map. A thick red arrow pointed down at my feet to prove it. I was in the Central Square of a large foreign city, feeling very lost and overwhelmed by the prospect of finding my way around. I got lost repeatedly in the days that followed, but always seemed to find myself back at that map. There the thick red arrow pointed again to the ground beneath my feet: 'You are here'. And each time I returned it was with less of a sense of exhaustion and failure, and more of a relief of recognition. It was the safest place to start from.

'You are here' is the best possible advice for anyone starting to learn to pray. Praying is not a question of 'succeeding' and 'getting it right'. It is not even about achieving anything. It is about drawing near to the love of God. And the love that prompts and draws us to pray is the same love that meets and embraces us when we do.

We are full of 'shoulds' and 'oughts' when it comes to the Christian life, and the awareness of what *ought* to be can become a millstone of condemnation around our necks. 'Pray as you can and do not pray as you can't,' says one spiritual guide, 'Take yourself as you find yourself and start from there.'

The great gift of God's love is that he allows us to start from exactly where we are, just as we are. And on the complicated map called Life, beside 'YOU ARE HERE' and my big red arrow, is another message and another arrow, pointing right beside me, 'I AM HERE TOO!'

Against the current

Praying in silence and solitude is not easy. We will be swimming against a powerful tide. Walk down any High Street if you need reminding of how much we love to live in noise and bustle. The idea of spending much time alone is a strange one. All the pressure is to live energetically and vigorously on the outside of life. Have you ever heard a person described as a 'healthy *intro*vert?'.

Even Christians feel that 'real' commitment to Christ is shown by how many meetings we are 'seen' at. When one friend shared how they had managed to spend an evening in quiet prayer and reflection, the response was 'I'd love a few hours to myself!'. They were left feeling very selfish for what they had done. No wonder people often say they feel guilty for wanting to spend time in solitude with God.

14

Everything around us tells us that life is to be valued by what is seen to be done. We are part of a culture that has largely lost the art of withdrawing and reflecting on the deeper questions of life. And in our superficiality we have been using the noise and activity to cover over a void of neglect and emptiness within us. But the mushrooming interest in spirituality, prayer and meditation, wherever it is on offer, shows that the hunger is deep and growing.

Inner noise

My first encounter with silence and solitude was when I visited the Taizé Community in France. Taizé is an ecumenical community of monks. They come from all over the world and from all Christian traditions. Every year thousands of young people visit Taizé to join in its life of prayer, worship and shared life.

When I arrived we were invited to join a discussion group for the week. Surrounded by strange people and strange languages I opted for the last group on the list – in the Field of Silence. This was a field set apart from the rest of the camp-site where people could spend time in quiet. Pastoral care and a daily Bible study were provided by one of the Brothers, but apart from that you were left alone. My motives were rather mixed – two major attractions on a camp-site with 6,000 people were the separate toilets and separate eating facilities for those opting for silence.

But for all that, I felt a growing enthusiasm for the idea. I was responding to something that deep down I wanted to understand better. So in the warm

15

afternoon sunshine I saw down on the grass with my Bible and tried to still myself for God.

It didn't work. I was almost immediately overwhelmed by a torrent of random thoughts and feelings welling up from inside. I was drowned in a turbulent flood of noise that made all concentration impossible. I did not know such noise was in me! It was as if the act of being silent was like lifting a lid off my inner world. All kinds of clamour and voices poured out. They were powerful. Prayer and reading was hopeless. I felt desolate and exhausted. I stuck at it though, with some encouragement from the Brothers. For several days I wandered restlessly, attended the worship and wondered if it wasn't all a mistake to have ever tried. But after four days or so I became aware that the flood was slowing down. My sleep became more peaceful and refreshing. At last there were moments of genuine stillness when I found myself able, rather hesitantly, to pray.

The 'sifting silence'

You may be someone who finds silence quite natural. You may enjoy being on your own. But not everyone finds it so easy to get into, and for others of you it may be quite a struggle. If that is the case, don't give up – you are not a failure!

If you are spending time alone and in silence for the first time, it is important to realise that the kind of experience I have just described is not unusual or wrong. If our activity and business has been a way of avoiding deeper questions and concerns, then we may feel, for a while at least, as if we are standing in the path of a dam that has burst. We are often so cluttered inside with the accumulations of years – hopes and fears, plans and ideas, light and darkness – that the Holy Spirit has to first of all clear a space. In the Quaker tradition the presence of the Holy Spirit within us is described as a 'sifting silence'. It is disturbing to experience it, but this clearing work is deeply loving. Just because we feel in turmoil it does not mean that God is too! The neglect of our inner world may mean that a lot of suppressed energy is locked up within us. Its strength and vigour can be alarming when we meet it for the first time. The following story may express what is going on.

A PARABLE: *The Kingdom of God is like a person who had been keeping a large dog shut up in a room under his house for many years. He neglected it and never let it out. One day the door was opened and in the joy and relief of its freedom the dog burst out frenzied activity, running, jumping, barking and rushing everywhere! It seemed uncontrollable. It greeted its owner with such energy that the person was unsure if it was loving or attacking him! At times it was frightening. But the owner gave time to the dog and cared for it with regular exercise. It grew calm and its companionship and vitality became a great source of joy to its owner. He had discovered a new source of life within his house.*

In the depths of a rather damp wood in East Sussex is a small monastery where the monks live a silent life of prayer. They share the woods with an archery club, and I can imagine that nothing stimulates trust in God quite like the possibility of dramatic martyrdom! Their chapel is an unassuming building, and on my first visit I went and knelt there

17

for a while. I had an uncomfortable sensation that I can only describe as being spiritually undressed! It was a firm but loving stripping of my preoccupations and securities. On each subsequent visit it was the same. That chapel, so quietly worshipped and prayed in for many years, was soaked in the sifting, silent presence of the Holy Spirit.

True and false silence

Silence will always feel attractive in a noisy and complex world. As we go on to explore the place of silence in Christian life and prayer it is important to recognise that some other forms of meditation and prayer appeal to the instinct to escape. Sometimes Christian prayer falls into the same trap. It is possible to manufacture all sorts of psychic and spiritual states of stillness and peace. They work like a drug, artificially damping down the demands and stress of the world outside. That is not the prayer and solitude that Jesus teaches us. Just because we *feel* quiet and close to God, doesn't mean that we actually are. Christian peace and prayer is not the absence of some*thing* (stress, pain, conflict etc.), but the presence of Some*one* with us in the midst of it all. In fact Christian prayer is drawing our lives more closely to the way of the cross. It is all about following the way of Christ.

It is therefore sad to find Christians who are resisting their intuitive desire to seek prayer in solitude because they feel it is selfish and escapist. Clearly, when the Holy Spirit guides our journey in prayer, it will be anything but an escape.

18

Starting out

Let us recap. We have found somewhere to be alone. We have 'closed the door'. We have begun to be still and prayed the simple refrain on our breathing, 'Lord Jesus Christ – have mercy on me.' But one thing is certain. It won't just be God who comes to fill our solitude. It may in fact feel as if God is the person who is *not* there!

The important thing is to resist the temptation to measure our progress in prayer and silence by 'how I am feeling'. The presence and work of God in our lives is something much deeper than feelings. Of course, feelings *are* important, but they are unreliable guides as to whether we are 'getting anywhere' in God's presence. Our emotions and passions need as much converting as the rest of us. Something much more profound is going on. In the solitude we will discover to our surprise that we are beginning to meet our selves and our world in a new way. It will be exciting and perhaps a bit frightening. We must choose how we respond.

Meeting our selves

I noticed a while ago that whenever I went away for a few days retreat three things always happened. When I began to lead retreats and quiet days myself, it was a relief to discover that I wasn't alone in my experience. It seems to be a common pattern.

The first thing to happen was that I kept falling asleep everywhere. This was an indication of the pace and tensions I had been living with. There in the quiet I was like a string puppet whose controls had been suddenly relaxed and I slumped to the floor. If that happens we need to be realistic and gentle with ourselves. Until we are refreshed we won't be able to take in anything else, let alone concentrate on God.

The second thing I noticed was that I developed a vast appetite for food! This was partly boredom no doubt. But perhaps, suddenly faced with these wide empty spaces of solitude and stillness, my eating was an instinctive reaching for comfort and 'filling'. However, we do not grow in Spirit by neglecting our human needs. When Elijah entered the desert exhausted and deeply in need of renewal, God first of all ministered to him by letting him sleep and by sending an angel with food! (1 Kings 19:4–8).

Thirdly, after a little while in silence, I would begin to get very restless and irritable. This is a very common reaction to being alone in silence. We have cut across our normal busy lives and stopped for a while. After some sleep and refreshment our natural response is to get moving again – and instead we are here in this empty space. Time alone like this refuses us all our usual securities, our ways of achieving and feeling we are useful. Here there is no one to chatter with, no television, no telephone to cover up the emptiness.

We are left feeling rather disarmed and powerless. We are out of control. It is actually rather frightening and so our natural response is to get angry. We will latch it on to the nearest available target – our room (which is freezing), the food (which is inedible), or the Retreat leader (whose talks are rubbish)! All of which may be true. But our real struggle is with facing our selves. This solitude and silence is assaulting all our ideas of 'usefulness'. It is inviting us to surrender our own small worlds and our pre-occupations. We are being drawn into something much bigger than ourselves. Solitude humbles us. In its own way it says to us, 'You are here'. This is where we start from – and all these hopes, insecurities, emptiness, and frustrations are the raw materials of who we are. We need to find a way of offering them to the renewing, recreating work of God.

Offering our selves.

Perhaps you were taught to deal firmly with 'distractions' when praying. Certainly it is a help to keep a notebook nearby so that when we remember that 'vital' phone call, we can jot it down and set it aside. But the word 'dis-traction' means far more than wandering thoughts. It literally means 'pulled apart'. What our scatty thoughts express in most of us is a much deeper fragmenting of who we are – our wills, our longings, our identity. There must be a place, carefully and lovingly, for listening to our dis-tractions and hearing what they are trying to say to us. It is important to realise that all these noises and voices and restlessness within are part of us and our world. In solitude we allow all those fragments to come before us. If we only treat them as nuisances or enemies we are rejecting people and situations that are part of us. Furthermore they must, in some way be important to us or they wouldn't keep coming to mind. We have not come into solitude to escape from our world. In solitude we will learn to love it all more truly. The way to God's presence is never by rejection, but by love.

One suggestion I have always found helpful. After

praying the simple focusing prayer that we learned in the last chapter, spend a moment gathering together your world – the clamour of voices, questions and tensions that fill your life at this time. You may open your hands as if you hold them all there. Accept them all as part of your world (even if you wish some of them weren't). Instead of pushing them aside, lovingly lift them up in your hands – offer them to God. Ask him to take and keep them and give you the space and grace to grow in love for them.

The mystery of our selves

When we give ourselves to God we are offering something we do not fully know or understand. The work of Carl Jung, the great psychoanalyst, has given new understanding into just how deep and complex human personality actually is. The greater part lies hidden from the surface of life most of the time. It also lies hidden from our own conscious memory. He wrote of the 'shadow' side of our personalities – the side that lies behind the 'Me' I offer to the world. It is in shadow because it is unseen not because it is necessarily sinister or to be feared. But Jung believed that the process of human maturing and personal wholeness had to include a meeting and integration of all sides of our personality. The idea is close to the teaching of Jesus. Jesus lived out of the full height and depth of human joy and pain, light and darkness, life and death.

A simple example might be the anger that I mentioned surfacing during the silent retreat. When you had planned to pray and concentrate on loving God that kind of raw and aggressive emotion can be very distressing; 'I shouldn't feel like this.' But we have already suggested that it may be important to listen to what the anger is saying and to offer it to God. At its deepest source, anger is a rich, creative, passionate energy. Though it comes out of our shadows we need it. It is God-given, and it needs transforming not denying.

The Bible teaches that there is a secret place deep within each of us where all of us must learn to live. It is place where all the diverse and dis-tracted parts of who we are, seen and unseen, can be unified and brought together into a single whole. This the Bible calls 'the heart'. To 'love the Lord your God with all your heart' is to love with your whole being united from its deepest place in one focus of devotion and adoration.

Our search for God is a search for that centre – for the heart and source of our lives. One writer expressed it like this, 'If a man is to turn his heart towards God, he must first of all *return* to his heart, from which he is so often absent. It was only after he had come back to his heart that the prodigal son could set out on the return of his Father. For man's true home is in the inmost depths of his heart.'[1]

When we are willing to wait in solitude and silent prayer before God, the Holy Spirit begins to re-centre our lives, picking through all the dis-tracted fragments and confusion, to the heart of who we are, to the place where God's love waits to welcome us. There we wait in hope and longing for the unfolding of the great secret, kept in God's love – the secret of who we are, in the image of the One who created us.

In the end, the decision to give our lives to Christ

and to seek him in prayer and solitude, is the decision to trust him with that secret – the secret of who we are becoming.

'We do not know what we shall become,' says John, 'but we know that when he [Christ] appears, we shall be like him' (1 John 3:2).

For reflection

There is much more to us than meets the eye, and if we can be a mystery to others at times, we are also a mystery to ourselves – faced with the frustrating, glorious and bewildering complexity that I call my 'Self'.

Meditate on these verses:

It was you who created my inmost self,
and put me together in my mother's womb;
for all these mysteries I thank you:
for the wonder of myself, for the wonder of your
works.
(Ps. 139:13–14, *Jerusalem Bible*)

Take a sheet of paper and mark a large circle. That is the whole of YOU. Mark in it some of your important relationships – past and present. Mark your personal qualities and characteristics (be honest!). Mark some of the important events in your life – the good and the bad. Mark your present activities. Mark some of your future hopes and anxieties.

Offer your personal world to God and share with him your honest feelings about your 'self'.

If you are discussing this in a group, it may be helpful to share your personal 'worlds' with each other, praying and encouraging each other as you do so. This needs a degree of trust and, of course, should not be forced.

Whenever you pray it helps to have a notebook beside you. You can keep a note of things that come especially to the fore in the silence. We can be very forgetful without such a discipline. With a notebook we can reflect on the significance of what was surfacing. Do take the opportunity to talk to a friend or pastor if it will help.

For reasons of temperament or past experiences, some people may be rather vulnerable in solitude and silence. All the ideas in this book are intended for people who are part of a regular church life of worship, prayer and Holy Communion. Christian prayer leads us into fellowship, and fellowship leads us back into prayer. It is important not to separate the two.

THREE

MEETING OUR WORLD

If you go into the desert because you don't like people, you will only lock yourselves up with a crowd of devils!

Thomas Merton

It is in solitude that I find the gentleness with which I am truly to love my brothers . . . Solitude and silence teach me to love my brothers for what they are, not for what they say.

Thomas Merton

He sat on a rickety old chair in a very bare and very cold 'guest' room. An old cloak was wrapped tightly round his worn habit. We talked about life and the Christian faith. I was full of ideas, books, causes and campaigns to change the world. He was a monk, living in this enclosed monastery, rarely leaving it and spending his days in silence and prayer – no newspapers, no television, no 'necessities' of life. But as we talked I found in him a shrewd wisdom, a quiet perception of life that was hard to believe. By any measure of 'normal' living he should have been totally out of touch.

And the more we talked, the more my own activities and enthusiasms began to feel very shallow beside this man. Quite clearly, in ways I could not comprehend, he was more deeply alive and involved in the world than I was.

Alone with God we meet our selves at a new depth. Alone with God we also meet the world around us in a deeper way. Solitude is not separation. Perhaps we know this better than we realise, for even when we pray the Lord's prayer on our own we still begin '*Our* Father . . .' Christian prayer is never private. It will always be personal for each of us, but in a very profound sense we never pray alone. This is part of what we mean when we speak of 'the communion of the saints'.

Getting alone can never really be an escape – at least, not for long. It may provide much needed space and rest, but that is not the same as flight. In fact real escape is impossible. As Thomas Merton warned, 'If you go into the desert because you don't like people, you will only lock yourself up with a crowd of devils!'[1] The truth is that we are, for better or worse, part of the world and our solitude will increase our awareness of our partnership – the joy and the pain of it. We will learn to love and respond to the world in a deeper way.

Detachment from the world

If solitude is not separation from the world, it does teach us a certain detachment from it. Detachment is not lack of interest. It is about learning to give space. Mature love is love that has learned to care and offer itself without taking over or possessing.

27

We meet such a love in Christ. In his love we are not dominated. His love delights in drawing out of each us our own uniqueness but he leaves us free to return his love to the glory of the Father.

Detachment enables us to stand back. It enables us to gain a wider perspective. It is not the withdrawal of love and involvement, but a more careful and discerning offering of it. Without detachment a sensitive love for this world, in all its complexity and pain, will be overwhelmed and drained empty.

A nun described how she came to a point where reading the daily newspapers, and watching television news on the state of the world, filled her with deep pain and agony of spirit. When she sought help she was advised, to her horror, not to watch the news or read the newspapers for a whole year! She protested that as a Christian nun she should be in touch with the needs of the world. How else could she pray with understanding? Her counsellor replied, 'You don't need to have all the details of the world's evil, to know the evil itself . . . you will meet it in prayer . . . learn to meet it in the depths and not simply in its surface forms'.[2]

Solitude is not separation. It awakens us to our deepest belonging in the joy and pain of the world.

Loneliness and solitude

Perhaps in your own times alone in prayer you feel you have had glimpses of this sense of belonging in the world. But it may equally be that the silence feels very empty and bleak. Is it our emptiness or the emptiness of the world around us? Does it matter which it is in the end? The Bible tells us that we are

28

part of a deeply divided and distracted world. The result of the first sin was separation. However, it may be that we avoid being alone for one of the simplest reasons, because it is lonely. Solitude faces us with our emptiness and the tedium of our own company.

We are often painfully unimaginative on the subject of loneliness. When we pray in church for the 'old, the sick and the lonely', what are we really saying? Is loneliness just the fate of an unfortunate minority? Are the young, healthy and married never lonely? The truth is that youthfulness, friendship and love are contexts in which we experience our humanity and longings. They are gifts of God on the road to wholeness. There is a danger in thinking that these 'contexts' can be solutions to the emptiness within that we fear. If we hide in them from loneliness we are in trouble. As Henri Nouwen writes:

When our loneliness drives us away from ourselves into the arms of our companions in life, we are, in fact, driving ourselves into excruciating relationships, tiring friendships and suffocating embraces. No friend or lover, no husband or wife, no community will be able to put to rest our deepest cravings for unity and wholeness . . . until we realise this we will be burdening others with these divine expectations.[3]

Loneliness is part of being human. It is being part of a dislocated world that longs to find its way back to God. There is mercy in the ache of loneliness, because it makes us reach out. It reminds us that we are not complete in ourselves. The one thing that was not 'good' in the Garden of Eden, was the loneliness of Adam. Out of that hunger he opened himself to his world and through his world, to Eve.

In the same way we are called to grow through loneliness into solitude.

For a number of years I lived and worked in a large Christian community at the Lee Abbey conference centre in north Devon. As new community members joined I could see myself again in the way they responded with excitement to the vision and joy of Christian love and belonging. It was powerful and real, and for a while it had a way of carrying people along. But for most of us there came a point, sooner or later, when it seemed to let us down. Feet touched solid ground again and, with that, there often came feelings of disillusionment and loneliness. The challenge at that time was to begin to find our own place and individuality in the fellowship, no longer being carried along on the corporate energy of the community. It was a kind of growing up. As Dietrich Bonhoeffer taught in his book *Life Together*, we can only live together when we have learned the freedom to be alone.

The experience itself was a very lonely one. But it was an important place to arrive at. It was important to realise that it was a place that could be made an offering to God in his service. In fact there is no experience of life that can't be offered in the same way. Thomas Merton wrote of a time when he suffered from insomnia and spent hours awake at night unable to sleep. He saw that the solitary emptiness and frustration of those hours could be made an offering of prayer to God.

Insomnia can become a form of contemplation. You just lie there, inert, helpless, alone, in the dark, and let yourself be crushed by the inscrutable tyranny of time. The plank bed becomes an altar and you lie there without trying to understand any longer in what sense you can be called a sacrifice. Outside in the world, where it is night, perhaps there is someone who suddenly sees that something he has done is horrible. He is most unexpectedly sorry and finds himself able to pray . . . [4]

A deeper love for others

After leaving Lee Abbey I spent two months in the silence and solitude of a cabin in the mountains of Switzerland. Five years so intensely involved with people had left me very tired. I was also uncertain as to what should come next. I knew I had to get alone, and opportunity was given.

There I began to experience something of the journey from loneliness to solitude. Loneliness feels that emptiness within is a place to be filled. In our hunger we devour friends and things around us. Solitude is the discovery that the emptiness within is a place from which we can reach out in love and welcome.

We experience loneliness in all sorts of ways. In that Alpine cabin there were times I acutely felt my lack of a phone. Unable to face the tedium of my own company I would have inflicted it on someone else. I had no television to fill up an evening. I could no longer surrender to the 'tyranny of diversion' in ways I was used to doing. I had to face simply being alone. But out of the tears and the pain of that emptiness there came a deeper awareness of my friends. There were times when they were more present to me than if I was with them physically. Truly, this solitude was not separation, but a meeting at a deeper level.

At the same time I was made more aware of my selfishness in love. I began to recognise patterns in my own friendships. With shame I remembered the times I had used people for my own ends. But there in the solitude love grew and friendships deepened. And as they did so, I sensed my own need to cling and possess was losing its grip and beginning to fade.

Thomas Merton put this experience into words for me when he wrote,

> It is in solitude that I find the gentleness with which I am to truly love my brothers. The more solitary I am the more affection I have for them. It is pure affection, and filled with reverence for the solitude of others. Solitude and silence teach me to love my brothers for what they are, not for what they say.[5]

It seems strange to speak of learning to love by being apart from people rather than being with them. But real love needs a capacity to separate as well as to be together. One of the hardest lessons at any stage of life is to love without possessing. Solitude has a disturbing way of laying bare our motives for loving. If we are willing to recognise them for what they are, we can confess them and let them go. And in that letting go a new source of loving can be released within us – the Spirit of God's love for all that he has made.

A deeper love for the world

Alongside my awareness and love for particular friends, was a growing love for the world itself. This was unexpected. Once a day in the Alps I listened to the World Service news on the radio. I then tried to pray for some of the issues I had just heard about. That summer the Gulf War was at a particularly brutal and dangerous stage. There were also atrocities by both sides in Northern Ireland and desperate famine in large areas of Africa. In the quiet of that alpine cabin, rather than feeling remote and rather sheltered from it all 'out there', I found myself praying with new involvement. I have never found intercession easy and I surprised myself by the energy with which I prayed. It no longer seemed to matter whether I was praying 'Lord have mercy on *me*,' or 'Lord have mercy on this world'. It was, in the end, the same prayer – together we stood in need of the salvation of God.

Many Christians are not really sure what their relationship should be with the world 'out there'. I was no exception. Out of misplaced loyalty to Christ and his Kingdom, my attitude to 'the world' (that is, outside the church) lurched self consciously between aggressive judgement to fearful wariness. Now, in the solitude, I became aware that I was deeply a part of the world. I was beginning to love what I had previously held at a distance. In truth, our love and searching for Christ must take us ever deeper into the heart of our world, for that is the path he chose into his Kingdom. So, for the first time, there were tears of pain for the empty food bowls of people I had never met or seen, and tears of joy for the announcement of a further nuclear arms reduction agreement.

The smile of God

If the silence of solitude, and the Spirit's presence there, exposes us to our emptiness and the poverty of our loving, it is only to lead us to the vitality and joy of God's love. In a tough sermon to his disciples on the cost of discipleship and the need to trust absolutely in what he has taught them, Jesus kept returning to joy and love as the heart of his message to them. 'I have told you all this so that my own joy may be in you and that your joy may be complete . . . Love one another as I have loved you.' (John 15:11–12). In that little alpine cabin there were many times of loneliness and emptiness, but there were moments when love would break through, so filling the moment that the sky itself became the smile of God and the wind his laughter in the wild joy of living. In such moments you can dare to believe that the gospel is really true and that in the end nothing will resist its life.

One gift in my solitude I will never forget. One morning I was reading from Luke's gospel. It was the story of Jesus bringing a little girl back to life (Luke 8:49–56). It is a moving story, and in Mark's account (5:35–43) he records the Aramaic words that Jesus actually spoke to the girl – *'Talitha koum!'* ('little girl, arise!'). I know a little girl called Talitha, who was named after that child. She and her younger brother Nathan are special friends of mine. Kneeling on the floor in my little wooden cabin in the mountains I remembered them both and naturally went

34

on to pray for my other God-children. Suddenly in the silence I saw Tally and Nathan running towards me, laughing and giggling and full of mischievous secrets. I felt I could almost touch them and I wept for the joy of loving them.

Some months later, I visited the family. I rang the front door bell and heard sounds of great excitement inside. Dad opened the door and there came Tally and Nathan towards me just as I had seen them in the Alps.

For reflection

Just as we are called to accept our selves before God, so we must accept our world.

In silence reflect on your world at this time – its priorities, its pressures, the good and the bad.

Open your hands as if you hold your world there and lift it up to God.

There may be things in your world you are rejecting or resisting, perhaps for a good reason. Are there practical things you can do in response to your prayer of acceptance – perhaps a talk with a friend, or an attitude to repent of?

Take a sheet of paper and mark a large circle. This is your world. Mark in it the important relationships, your home and local community. Put in your interests and favourite TV programmes. Mark in the events of the wider world that catch your attention at the moment – its joys and its pains.

Reflect upon your world and those who share it

with you. Pray for them and ask God's blessing on them.

If you are in a group, it may be helpful to share your world and pray for a deepening awareness of it in God's love.

F O U R

RETURN TO THE HEART

The desperate need today is not for a greater number of intelligent people, or gifted people, but for *deep* people.

Richard Foster

Unless you can find God in the secret place of the heart in the midst of everyday noise and business, then physical solitude will be threatening and negative.

Brother Ramon

A monk went to an older monk in the desert and asked him for advice. Though deeply committed to God and prayer he was still dissatisfied. The older monk replied, 'Go and sit in your cell, and your cell will teach you everything.'[1]

Anything else would be easier, wouldn't it? 'Go and read this marvellous book', 'go and talk to. . . .', go and *do* anything. But to stop – this is death. It involves a letting go of our usual sources of meaning and value and security. It is stopping the world. It means being willing to sit in emptiness. It means, by our own standards of measuring life, being 'useless' and 'wasting time'. No wonder we avoid it. But our resistance to it is, in the end, a resistance to truth.

However, the kind of solitude we have been exploring is not meant to be a sentence of death, but the gift of God himself. It is the place where the gift of life is freed to be deepened, broadened and above all transfigured in the joyful mystery of God's love. The solitude of Jesus, as we have already seen, was the place where his life 'came together'. For him solitude was a constant returning to the heart.

Jesus taught that our lives must be lived in the power and presence of the Spirit. The work of the Spirit is to lead us 'into all truth'. So it will not be surprising if there are times when solitude becomes a place of disturbing and painful exposure – to ourselves, to our world, to our God. But all this is to bring us to a place of rich and joyful encounter with God.

Thrown together with solitude

Do we choose solitude or does solitude choose us? People sometimes speak of feeling quietly pursued by God. Others feel that they are the ones doing to pursuing. One lovely Celtic blessing captures both sides of this mutual search when it closes with the lines, 'I on the path of God, God upon my track.'

Many of the most well known characters in the Bible were people whose lives were shaped at some stage by time alone with themselves and with God. In most cases it was not an experience that they chose for themselves; it was more often a place where they ended up. The experience of Elijah following his triumph on Mount Carmel has always spoken most directly to my own experience. This is probably because, like most stubborn people, I only learn my deepest lessons through a crisis.

Elijah was one of the greatest spiritual leaders and prophets in the Bible. Even Jesus was confused with him at times (Mark 8:27–8). As Jesus cried out from the cross, some assumed he was calling Elijah to rescue him (Mark 15:35–6). But in 1 Kings, chapter 19, we meet a very human and vulnerable man. Elijah is alone, exhausted and frightened, having fled into the desert for fear of his life. Only days before he had single-handedly triumphed over four hundred and fifty prophets on Mount Carmel. It had been an astonishing demonstration of confident faith and the power of God.

The significant point about his crisis was that it was a problem of strength not weakness. His was a problem of success not failure. His very faithfulness had brought him to this point. But now he has run out. He wants to die. He has had enough.

The borders of solitude

Elijah finds himself all alone in the desert, bitter and desolate. In terms of the deeper journey his flight represents, he has come to the borders of solitude. But he has come by way of his own exhaustion, not through choice. It feels like death – and he wants to die (19:4).

In less dramatic ways, this story of Elijah is retold wherever people give themselves sacrificially to the service of God. One observation from involvement with the wide range of Christians who came to Lee Abbey, for a holiday or retreat, was the high level of tiredness that people seemed to assume had to go with Christian service. And those whose tiredness was most neglected were those who had managed to 'keep going' in spite of it. It is one of the most frequent areas of neglect – the care for the 'strong' in our churches. It is all too easy to assume that because they are keeping going they must be all right.

Often the most tired, most isolated and discouraged were not those who had experienced failure in their Christian lives. Things had not gone especially wrong for them. They were those whose strength had run out in the course of loving and faithful service. And now, in a desert of their own weariness, they were adding to their pain by accusing their emptiness of being failure and weakness. The important thing at this stage was to recognise the message that the crisis brought with it.

While we have the strength to keep going we are often our own worst enemies. It means that the point of stopping and facing the exhaustion within can feel very overwhelming. We have been denying it for so long. We have been seeking our securities in compulsive activity. But now we feel we have entered a desert place, barren and desolate. It is hard to believe at such times that this silent and shadowy wasteland could be the home of the Spirit, concealing the deepest springs of God's life and our security. Surely this is a place to avoid rather than journey further into? Our natural longing is to look back to the life we have lost.

These things I remember as I pour out my soul:
how I used to go with the multitude,
  leading the procession to the house of God,
with shouts of joy and thanksgiving
  among the festive throng.

Why are you so downcast, O my soul?
Why so disturbed within me?   (Ps. 42:4–5)

Back in the wilderness with Elijah (19:5–7), we read
that he first sleeps, then eats some food and sleeps
again. Then, simply and directly, God comes to
Elijah, and the pain and anguish of his exhaustion
is allowed to surface (19:10) – it must be given voice.
Elijah feels bitterly let down after all he has given to
God and his people. He expresses his anger. (Notice
again the three-fold pattern of sleep, food and anger
that often marks the entry into times of silence and
prayer.)

Now God comes in a different way to Elijah
(19:11–13). First the whirlwind, but God is not in
the whirlwind. Next an earthquake, but God is not
in the earthquake. Thirdly fire, but God is not in
the fire. And when all this sound and fury has swept
past Elijah, there is 'a gentle whisper'. This has
traditionally been translated 'a still small voice', but
it is not a voice at all that is described here. The
meaning is closer to 'the sound of silence'.

The fire, earthquake and whirlwind were all signs
of the power and drama of Elijah's ministry up to
that time. But now, God is not in them. And without
God they are worthless and empty. God is reminding
Elijah that the roots of his identity, security and
strength must penetrate beneath and beyond the

surface of life – into the silence and solitude of God himself.

Jesus himself experienced great signs and wonders as part of his ministry. But before and after each point of giving out he withdrew. He chose solitude. And in that solitude his life and ministry were renewed.

Returning to the centre

As Elijah's story unfolds, he is taken on a journey. He has travelled from Mount Carmel to Mount Horeb. This is a deeply symbolic journey. He has journeyed from the mountain of his own achievement to the mountain of God (Horeb is the range of mountains that includes Mount Sinai). In journeying to this holy mountain, the mountain of God's revelation and law-giving, Elijah has returned to the centre and heart of his own faith.

Finally, God speaks directly to Elijah's sense of loneliness and isolation. He had thought he was completely alone, but God assures him that, although the path continues to be costly and dangerous, he remains part of a large fellowship of faithful believers (19:18). So he learns that his solitude, though costly, is not separation. And in that context, God once again sends him out into the world with a job to do.

Disturbing the comfortable

After preaching on this story once I was approached by a Christian who had been forced to flee his own

42

country for fear of his life. He spoke very movingly of how deeply he had come to identify with this period in Elijah's life. He shared with me something of the anguish and isolation he had felt at that time. 'Let me tell you', he said, ' "I even I only am left, and they seek my life that they might kill me" – let me tell you, there is no despair like that.' When I heard that testimony I realised that I had been guilty of drawing only 'spiritual' meaning from the story. But for Elijah, as for many persecuted Christians in the world today, it was a matter of life and death. There are many testimonies of Christians, who have learned to root their lives in the secret heart of God's presence. And by doing so they have endured all kinds of imprisonment, and human isolation.

Of course most of us with the freedom to read these pages face no such direct threat to our lives. Perhaps the perils we face are more subtle. In his book *Celebration of Discipline*, Richard Foster wrote, 'Superficiality is the curse of our age. The doctrine of instant satisfaction is a primary spiritual problem. The desperate need today is not for a greater number of intelligent people, or gifted people, but for *deep* people.'[2] In such an indulgent and self-sufficient culture there is surely mercy at work in anything that breaks through to our depths, provoking a crisis that reminds us that we are created for more than 'this'. As someone once put it, 'Christ comes to comfort the disturbed, and *disturb the comfortable*'.

The call to solitude is the call to centre our lives deeply and radically in the heart of God alone. It is not a rejection of activity or business as such. Solitude will give our lives a firm foundation. From such a base the pressures and demands of life won't sweep us away. It is, in the end, the deepest work of conversion to which we can give ourselves for the sake of the Gospel. It begins with the willingness to wait in the emptiness, in hunger and thirst. It ends with the divine gift of God.

This was the secret of Jesus' strength and vision. It must be the source of the life of his followers also.

Ideas for solitude

We began by suggesting that time alone should be the way we punctuate the activity of our lives. Punctuation is what draws out of a piece of writing its fullest meaning and purpose. Solitude, time alone, is a way of pacing and interpreting our activity in the light of God's love and will for us.

This section closes with some ideas for 'punctuating' our lives. Of course people vary enormously in terms of personality, lifestyle and commitments. The following suggestions may help you to make a practical response in a way that is appropriate to you at the moment. It may also help to talk through the possibilities with a friend.

One further point to make. If your diary is already cluttered, it will do no good trying to squeeze in 'space for God' as another commitment. You may first have to ask the question, 'What am I going to give up to make this possible?'

PUNCTUATION MARKS

Daily and weekly: Are there times and places where I could punctuate my day or week with moments of stillness, pausing, drawing breath, listening to God?

44

Finding space first thing in the morning is not practical for everyone. For some people the journey to and from work can be a good opportunity. It may help to use some of the prayer exercises suggested at the end of each chapter. The lunch break may offer a once-a-week chance to sit in a local church or in a park.

It may even be possible at work itself. When I started writing this book I was actually working full time as a dish washer in a hospital kitchen. It was noisy, hot and monotonous, and at times bored me to distraction. But there were other times when I found myself learning to offer the moment to God and discovered, to my surprise, that the stillness of solitude was possible even there.

If you are at home there may be times in the day when you can stop and 'centre on God'? Meal times make a natural stopping point for some people. Why not light a candle and just sit quietly as you eat – without the television or radio.

I know of couples who every so often take turns at caring for the children in order to give a few hours space for the other. Sometimes a room in a friend's house can prove an easier place to be quiet, without distraction from the phone for example. But don't assume that children are incapable of being quiet. It is from adults they learn that noise is better – consider how hard adults work to get a noisy response from children when they meet them. Very rarely do we sit quietly with children and let them sense our joy and love for them in stillness.

One useful resource for these pauses in the day is to have a small notebook in which you have written down verses of scripture, prayers, poems and reflections – anything that helps to give you a starting point in the silence.

Longer intervals: some people block a day a month, or every other month in their diaries, for a longer period of quiet. Some churches organise Quiet Days for their congregation. (A great gift to every Christian church would be a file containing a list of addresses and practical details of local places where people can go for short or long periods of quiet and prayer. Some sources of information are given in the Notes at the end of this book.)[3]

At least once a year we should aim to get away for longer than a day. Two nights minimum. But again, it is important to be practical and to do what we can, not what we can't. It is certainly true that at particular points in our lives, for practical and good reasons, such time away may not be possible. But it is also true that many other people could go on retreat and do not.

The saddest deterrent from going on retreat is when church activities make it 'impossible'. If work *for* God is stopping us being *with* God, then we need to take a hard look at our priorities.

For longer periods of time most of us would need someone to guide and lead us in the silence. These days there are many places around the country offering retreats of varying length and style. They report a spectacular rise in numbers of people coming to them. And because many of those coming are new to the experience of silence and spending extended time in prayer, these retreat centres are very sensitive to people who are trying it for the first time.

John Pearce's booklet, *Advance by Retreat*,[4] is a very helpful introduction for those thinking about

46

retreats or quiet days for the first time. He answers many of the practical questions. Brother Ramon's *Deeper into God*[5] is a helpful resource book for actually using such times. It is full of ideas, Bible-reading and suggested structures for the day.

Remember that it is not *quantity* of time that matters, but *quality*. Living and praying have become so separated in our culture and experience that our efforts on the Underground or at the kitchen sink tend to feel second best. In fact Brother Ramon, in his book *A Hidden Fire*, makes the point that these are among the best places to begin to seek solitude. 'Unless you can find God in the secret place of the heart in the midst of everyday noise and business, then physical solitude will be threatening and negative.'[6]

For reflection

Reflect on the seasons of the natural world – the seasons of dying, rising, fallow and growth, sowing and harvest. Which are your favourite seasons? Do you know why?

Reflect on the Christian year – the seasons of the Church in the life of Christ – the 'punctuation' through the year with which we express our worship, penitence, celebration and prayer. Which seasons mean the most or the least to you? Do you know why?

Reflect on the seasons of human life. If you are in a group with people of different ages, consider how attitudes to silence and reflection vary. For example, the silence of a elderly person may express a sense of fullness and rest at the end of life. Consider the silence of children fascinated by what they are looking at. Equally, our silences may reflect times of pain or bewilderment or loneliness.

Take some time to consider the 'seasons' of your own life. On a sheet of paper draw the peaks and the troughs of your own life-journey so far. There may have been times of spring – of growth and fullness and achievement. There may have been times of autumn and winter – of fruitfulness but also of death and disappointment. Reflect on how you feel about the way your life has unfolded. If it is appropriate, share it with a group or with a friend, and pray together over the insights that come to light.

You may also consider the 'seasons' of your year. Of course, no one year is 'typical'. Life changes too fast for that. But on a sheet of paper look back over the last twelve months. Mark the seasons – the times of special busy-ness or pressure, the times of rest and holiday. Mark the anniversaries and times of special memory or celebration. Look for the times and seasons at the heart of your life, where you are refreshed and renewed with God's love and life. Are they there? Once again, it may be helpful to share this with a friend or in your group.[7]

PART II

THE COMPANIONSHIP OF SILENCE

FIVE

A PREFERENCE FOR THE DESERT

Yahweh is first and foremost, a God of the Wilderness.

Kenneth Leech

As a deer pants for streams of water,
so my soul pants for you, O God.
My soul thirsts for God, for the living God.

Ps. 42:1–2

Christian prayer is a preference for the desert, for emptiness, for poverty.

Thomas Merton

Blessed are those who hunger and thirst for righteousness, for they will be filled.

Matt. 5:6

As the world was being created, the Jewish story goes, all the angels of God were busy with different tasks. To one was given the job of planting trees and sowing seeds throughout the earth. Another was sent with a huge carrier of water to distribute as oceans and rivers. Another was given an enormous bag of stones to spread round the world. And as he was flying over Israel – the bag split!

Anyone who has visited Israel will understand the wry humour in that story. There are stones and boulders everywhere. The heat and light and uncompromising terrain give the land a rugged intensity of life and spirit. Visit in different seasons and you will witness almost wild extremes of barrenness and fruitfulness, of death and life. Is it really all that surprising that the deserts and mountains of the Middle East should have given birth to three great world religions – Judaism, Christianity and later, Islam?

The way of life, worship and prayer taught in the Bible is a belief shaped and learned in the desert. Kenneth Leech, in his book *True God*, goes further when he writes, 'Yahweh is first and foremost a God of the Wilderness.'[1] It is these dry, solitary wastes that provide the Hebrew people with their most vivid imagery in prayer and worship:

> O God, you are my God
>> earnestly I seek you;
> my soul thirsts for you,
>> my body longs for you,
> in a dry and weary land
>> where there is no water.   (Ps 63:1)

The deepest roots of the faith in the Bible lie in the solitary, rugged silences of the desert. And throughout the Bible some of the greatest and most glorious revelations of God were in the wilderness. It was there that God first 'found' the people Israel (Deut. 32:10). It was there that God revealed his own Name and commandments (Exod. 3:2, 19:1ff). Many of the later prophets looked back with longing to the days of Israel's 'pure' faith in the desert (for example, Amos 5:25). And finally it is the place where the final glory of Israel will be revealed when the desert shall bloom with life (Isa. 35:1, 6). When John the Baptist came to prepare people to meet with Christ he called them into the desert (Mark 1:1–8 echoing the words of Isaiah). In doing so he called them out of the 'safety' of their familiar ground, back to the spiritual roots of their own faith. The priorities of life look very different when seen from the wastes of the wilderness. And it is here, say the prophets, that we will meet the living God in spirit and in truth.

The power of silence

One of the most overwhelming impressions on spending time in the mountains of Sinai and the deserts of Egypt, was the power of the silence. The intensity was alarming. There was an almost physical quality to it. It pressed upon me like the heat of the sun above. Across such silent wastes, I reflected, the people of Israel wandered and contemplated and struggled to understand the God who had rescued them. In such lonely terrain, Jesus himself wrestled with his calling and identity. The silence here was tough and searching but full of life. Resting in the shadow of a desert boulder, or climbing Mount Sinai in the heat of the day, silence, like an uncompromising but faithful companion, pursued me, questioning, probing, seeking truth. At other times, in the early morning or in the evening, the silence softened and yielded in a stillness that wove its presence round me like a seamless robe. There seemed to be no part of life that it didn't touch and influence.

The impact of the wilderness upon travellers from the more sophisticated and crowded cultures of the West is varied and often profound. In *A Journey in Ladakh*, Andrew Harvey beautifully described his first impressions of travelling high up in the wild, remote mountains of Tibet:

> As the bus creaked and wheezed its way slowly up that vast winding pass, I found my mind falling silent, becoming as empty as the spaces between the mountain faces, as wide as the skies above the peaks of the mountains. . . . That silence! It is the quality of that silence that no words can convey, that silence sustained over millennia, in which every sound and movement was contained, with which every object in that world was bathed, as if with shining water. I had never felt before as I felt on that day the transforming power of silence, its genius in giving everything back to itself.[2]

That last phrase, 'giving everything back to itself', particularly struck me. In the first section of this book we reflected on the power of solitude, guided by the Holy Spirit, to draw out of us both our own uniqueness in Christ and our profound belonging in the heart of all creation. So many things in life possess us and claim us for themselves. And in our turn we claim and possess others. What Andrew Harvey was intuitively sensing was the unique way that solitude and silence are places where all that can be untangled. We are given back to ourselves to start again.

In the early centuries of its existence the Christian Church remained close to the physical wilderness, spreading as it did along the trade routes of the Middle East and the Mediterranean coastlands. But with the conversion of the Emperor Constantine, Christianity became the institutional religion of the whole Roman Empire. At this time a significant number of Christians chose the desert. They withdrew into the desert for lives of solitary prayer and silence. It was not an organised movement, but individuals responded to what they felt to be a call for deeper prayer and waiting on God. Although it was not their intention or purpose, they became a highly influential source of counselling and guidance, and we know them as the Desert Fathers. It is all too easy to assume that, by doing this, they were running from the 'real world'. In fact they saw part of their calling as involving spiritual warfare and battle against evil in the world. Their writings and sayings show that their solitude and withdrawal was deeply rooted in God's guidance and will, and the impact they made on the 'real world' after their 'escape' was considerable. They were much sought out by people of their day, and collections of sayings and stories about them have circulated in the Church ever since. They were rugged, practical people of few words, shrewd discernment and down-to-earth wisdom.

One story catches something of the character of these men of God. It is a story that has been retold in different cultures and religious traditions. A young man sought out a solitary holy man, eager to talk to him about prayer. The old man said nothing but built up his small fire and made tea. He then began to pour the tea into the young man's cup. Though it was full he went on pouring. Tea spilled all over the ground. The young man finally protested: 'It's already too full!'

'So it is with you,' said the old man. 'Until you are empty, how can you receive what you seek?'[3]

Hunger and thirst for God

René Voillaume explains the significance of the desert like this:

> The desert bears in its physical reality the sign of isolation, not only from people and human life, but from any semblance of human activity and presence. Being something that man cannot put to use, it likewise bears the sign of aridity, and consequently the subduing of all the senses, including both sight and hearing. It also bears the sign of poverty and austerity, and most extreme simplicity. In short, it bears the sign of man's complete helplessness, as he can do nothing to subsist alone and by himself in the desert, and thus he discovers his weakness and the necessity of seeking help and strength in God.[4]

Commenting on this insight, Kenneth Leech adds, 'The Desert Fathers believed that the wilderness was supremely valuable to God precisely because it was valueless to man. There was nothing to exploit in the wasteland. So it was the natural dwelling place of the man who sought nothing but himself'[5] – and to find himself in God. The desert then is the place where we contemplate our limits, our finitude and our dependencies. For some this may all feel very morbid and introspective. Certainly, to be alone in the desert preoccupied with your self is hell. But that is not its object. There is no virtue in self-torture. Desert faith has had its share of eccentrics. At times it may have encouraged a form of discipleship that is a thinly veiled gesture of self-hatred and rejection, a loveless slavery. But if you read the Desert Fathers you will quickly discover they had no time for such spiritual heroics. Love is the way to God, not self-hatred or contempt for the world.

Desert faith and prayer does challenge an opposite and easier temptation. It is the complacent expectation that God exists to simply fill our world and meet our needs on request. In bringing us to a place of emptiness, of facing our hunger and thirst, the wilderness has a way of weaning us off our need for constant 'experiences' and 'consolations'. It teaches us to live by faith not by sight. This is not a rejection of 'experiences' of God, but the recognition that it is God we are called to trust in, not his gifts.

But all this stops short of the secret that inspired the silent prayer of the Fathers of the wilderness. They insisted that in the silence of desert prayer we do not just meet our own poverty and emptiness. We keep silence because it is, in the end, the only way we may draw near to the holy, unseen God. 'God', it has been said, 'is a friend of silence.' After all, what marked out this wilderness God of the Hebrews from the other deities around was that he could not be expressed. He was unseen. He dwelt in 'cloud and thick darkness' (Exod. 20:21). The other gods could all be seen. They were mere idols. But no art could express the likeness of the one true

God. No words could speak the final truth of him. He is, and dwells in, silence. When all our attempts to speak and describe have failed, there remains the desert of awe and loving silence, of communion, not communication. Words are not wrong, but we need to recognise their limits. Words can only take us so far in our understanding and meeting with God. Words are finite. Is it really so surprising that we should fall silent before such a God? Perhaps the real surprise is that we go on talking as much as we do. As Henri Nouwen wrote, 'Silence alone shares something of God's infinity.'[6]

Time and again it is the desert that gives words or pictures to God's people in their hopes and struggles. In Psalm 42, the deer panting in the wilderness, lifting its quivering nostrils in the hot breeze trying to catch the scent of water nearby, expresses all the poet's thirst and longing for God: 'so my soul pants for you, O God' (42:1). In his turmoil of faith he is 'unquiet' within. In Psalm 62 rocks and stones speak of the solid permanence of God's goodness through all troubles. 'My soul waits in silence for God, from him comes my salvation . . . from him comes my hope' (62:1, 5).[7] Here the silence is not a despairing, or helpless loss of words, but a waiting and trusting that is full of confidence and hope.

Emptying ourselves

It was in this spirit that Thomas Merton once described Christian prayer as 'a preference for the desert, for emptiness, for poverty'.[8] Yet to some this whole discussion about the desert may seem negative and depressing. But it is very close to the spirit of the

Sermon on the Mount. There Jesus gives a startling picture of the persons he regards as 'blessed'. They are poor, hungry and thirsty, meek, mourning, persecuted, yet merciful, pure in heart and able to bring peace. They are 'desert dwellers'. When we contemplate the call of the desert we are not simply looking at the way *some* Christians have learned to pray and chosen to live. We are contemplating the teaching and example of Jesus himself, who chose to root his own life in the solitary, silent wastes of the wilderness *in order to give himself to the world*.

The call to the desert is the call to empty ourselves, as Christ did; to live by a radically different source of life and security. 'Your attitude should be the same as that of Christ Jesus,' says Paul, 'who . . . emptied himself' (Phil. 2:5–7). Christian living and praying is to be a mutual self-emptying (*kenosis*) between us and God. God in Christ poured out into the world, we in our turn poured out, emptied into Christ for his service. Philip Seddon puts it movingly like this:

> There is a deeply humbling mutual exchange, a mutual *kenosis*, in all our dealings with God. Any costly generosity towards him on our part draws out of him a costly graciousness and an overwhelming mercy far in excess of what is 'necessary'.[9]

This is the way of desert prayer. This is the spirit in which to be silent before God.

For reflection

Read Psalm 63 or 42. Can you imagine the world the psalmist lives in? What pictures come to mind as you read it slowly?

We have considered the desert as a sign of human emptiness and dryness. If you are in a group, discuss where you think the modern 'deserts' are in our world today. Where are the places we experience our emptiness and helplessness.

Try writing your own psalm, using parts of your world and environment to express your longings and feelings?

SIX

THE FEARFUL VOID

. . . death could not hold him.

Acts 2:24

Lord Jesus Christ, Son of the living God, at this evening hour you rested in the tomb and so sanctified the grave to be a bed of hope to all believers . . .
Prayer from the late-night service of Compline

[Silence is] spring breaking up through the death of winter.

Sarah, in 'Children of a Lesser God'

Sarah: I live in a place you can't enter. It's out of reach.
James: Out of reach? That sounds romantic.
Sarah: Deafness isn't the opposite of hearing, as you think. It's a silence full of sound.
James: It's a silence full of sound?
Sarah: The sound of spring breaking up through the death of winter.[1]

James is a speech therapist and Sarah a deaf student. They fall in love and their story is told in the play, *Children of a Lesser God*. They meet when he is given the task of teaching her to speak. She refuses

61

to learn, arguing that signing is a better language than speaking and silence is not second best to sound and hearing. She is not the child of a 'lesser God'. James, the speech therapist is constantly left feeling powerless by the silence that surrounds their relationship. She can't even hear his jokes! It disarms him. He feels insecure in it. And she constantly complains that he is trying to change her. In one argument Sarah tries to explain her world and his pain in trying to draw near it.

The last line of the extract I have quoted stunned me when I heard it. What felt like death to James was life to Sarah. But to draw near in love and share her secret meant a kind of dying for him. He had never had to love this way before. He could no longer be in control. He had to surrender himself. But the invitation to surrender to the death of silence came with the promise of resurrection. Spring breaking up the death of winter.

Silence and death

Silence is often linked with death. In the Old Testament, before a belief in an afterlife began to emerge, the place of the dead, 'Sheol', was seen as a twilit, shadowy place of silence. Our Western culture too often experiences silence as a kind of deadness, a withdrawal of life. It is an absence, a privation. Some attitudes to silence may be peculiarly British. Where else in the world can you stand crammed, shoulder to shoulder in a railway carriage, in total silence! We have an ambivalence about silence much of the time. Although we may protest that 'all I want is some peace and quiet', we don't really want too much. Given an unexpected hour of space in the day we quickly get restless and try to fill it up. The space and emptiness of it unsettles us. 'I don't like it, it's too quiet,' is the stock line in any thriller or horror film. There the silence hints at a hidden menace, an un-named threat. Not surprisingly, silence is often used as a punishment. We threaten our children with it unless they behave. We impose it socially on people who have offended or upset us. Solitary confinement and silence has been used as an effective torture throughout history. In Paul Simon's song, 'Silence, like a cancer, grows', reflecting the decaying heart of a despairing, apathetic society where no one seems to be listening or concerned.

No wonder we are uncertain about it. But what lies at the heart of our unease? One writer suggests that to accept the companionship of silence must always mean a kind of death for us.

> In renouncing speech . . . we yield up something fundamentally human – a central means for declaring and expressing our existence. It is a kind of annihilation. Viewed this way, silence is equated with death. To discover that our lives are 'rooted in silence that is not death but life' one must first keep quiet. And keeping quiet entails anxiety.[2]

Death – companion and friend

The willingness to be silent, to 'enter the desert', requires a willingness to face death. Put like that it sounds terribly stark and negative. Isn't Christianity about life and joy? Yes, it is. But this gift of life comes through a profound conversion, a letting go, a dying to one life in order to receive another. Jesus was very clear that following him meant dying. 'If anyone would come after me, he must deny himself and take up his cross and follow me. For whoever wants to save his life will lose it, and whoever loses his life for me will find it' (Matt. 16:24–5). Dietrich Bonhoeffer put it bluntly, 'When Christ calls a man he bids him come and die.'

Bonhoeffer's final months of life were spent as a prisoner of the Nazis. He was finally executed in the last days of the war. Yet he wrote a series of meditations in prison called, 'Stations on the road to freedom'. In one of these he welcomed death as a place of Christian celebration:

> Come now, thou greatest of feasts on the journey to freedom eternal; death, cast aside all the burdensome chains, and demolish walls of our temporal body, the walls of our souls that are blinded, so that at last we may see that which here remains hidden.[3]

The Christian attitude to death is both one of acceptance and also of protest. It reminds us of our mortality. It must be accepted as the place where everyone must come eventually and surrender life. But in the name of Christ we protest its final claims upon us. It is also the place Christ has defeated by his resurrection. 'Death could not hold him' (Acts 2:24). Lying in his earthly tomb, sharing the death of our mortality, Christ has 'sanctified the grave to be a bed of hope to all believers'.[4]

St Francis was another saint for whom death was a celebration. Far from being a nameless terror encountered at the end of earthly life, 'Sister Death' was his constant companion and friend. She was a friend whose firm but loving wisdom kept the Christian moving towards the true securities and lasting goals of God's grace. In every moment of passing, of changing, of losing, of letting go, we die a little. And in the company of Sister Death, we are shaken a little freer to receive the gift of true life in God.

The hymn, 'All Creatures of our God and King', is based on the Canticle of the Sun attributed to St Francis. It is a popular hymn in Christian worship and often sung at weddings and other special occasions. This beautiful song celebrates the many seasons of life and creation and calls them to worship God. It contains the following verse,

> And thou, most kind and gentle death,
> Waiting to hush our latest breath,
> O praise him, alleluia,
> Thou leadest home the child of God,
> And Christ our Lord the way hath trod:
> O praise him, O praise him . . .

Because it is a long hymn and a verse is usually left out, I have never yet heard this verse sung in Christian worship. Death is always omitted.

While we try and live as if there is no death and dying, real living is impossible. We have made a stranger and enemy of one of the two certainties of mortal life – that we were born and we will die. We have also made an enemy of the place where we meet Christ in his greatest gift to us – his death on the cross. We live with a deep anxiety of death.

I was sitting recently at the bedside of a lady in her last hours of a long and remarkable earthly life.

For those few hours I sat, holding her hand, sometimes praying and reading the Bible, sometimes talking to the relative who was nursing her. Keeping vigil on the threshold of life and death, thoughts swing from the deep and profound, to the very practical and ordinary. There were moments when death felt very ordinary and matter-of-fact. Yes, there was grief and pain in parting, but it was part of the finite nature of things. But at other moments I found myself contemplating the amazing Christian claims we make regarding death. Our hope is that in this thing called death is the promise of life released and overwhelmingly transfigured in the glory of God's presence. Beside that frail, fading body hope and anxiety struggled within me. Is all this true? Am I close here to the reality of life transfigured. Or is this the end of life, the fearful void of death?

This question is actually more present in our lives than we care to admit. The uncertainties of daily life – its disappointments, failures and insecurities – all tap into the deeper, anxious questions of who we are, or who we are not. And so do the joys and blessings of life. It is not all exaggeration when we say we are 'so happy I could die', or find something so lovely we 'can't take any more'. We can die of laughing or of loving and often protest we are in danger of doing so. Both the heights and depths of human experience take us to our limits. They remind us of our finitude and our life in a finite creation.

Silence and eternity

Once again Andrew Harvey, in the wildness of the Tibetan mountains, expresses this beautifully:

I had never felt before . . . the transforming power of silence, its genius in giving everything back to itself. Each mountain existed in its unique contortion; each crag of purple rock, each landslide of scree, each winding dark stream, each small shrub clawing the sides of the road, each bird, seemed to be so full of its own essence that it hovered on the brink of dissolution, so brimming with energy that I feared often it could not survive itself, and I would not survive feeling its radiant danger, and my own, so acutely.[5]

In our willingness to be still and silent we are drawing near to death and to the boundaries of our human existence. But here we also discover that we have crossed over another frontier into the infinite love of God. Silence touches eternity. Death lies side by side with resurrection. Part of our wandering in the wilderness of silence is to make the journey through fear of death into a silence 'that is not death but life'. This is the spring that breaks up through the death of winter. For our death is the place of Christ's eternal victory. God has suffered all deaths and endings, and made an end a beginning. Death could not hold him. Death is now a companion on the way to life. Death has been converted to Sister Death, a companion-guide on the journey home. Thank God for death.

Letting go of God

The silence of Christian prayer is, therefore, a profound letting go into God. I want to suggest even that at times it involves a letting go *of* God. When

I made my home in an alpine cabin for two months I wanted to spend time with God. To my dismay the silence was empty. Even the most familiar comforts of faith and assurance were missing. It was a wilderness and I had no way of knowing how far it would stretch before me. I wept over God's absence. I protested and got very angry. I hammered on the walls of the cabin demanding his presence. This was a crisis of faith. How could I believe any more? Who was God anyway? And then I began to realise the nature of my demands. To my crying, 'Who are you?', the silence echoed, 'Who are *you*?. The temptation to negotiate with God runs so deep. I remembered the prayer of Thomas Merton in his early days as a monk when all his longing for God, poured out and passionate, seemed only to meet a deep and disarming silence.

> God, my God, God whom I meet in darkness, with you it is always the same thing! I have prayed to You in the daytime with thoughts and reasons, and in the night-time You have confronted me, scattering thought and reason. I have come to You in the morning with light and with desire, and You have descended upon me, with great gentleness, with most forbearing silence, in this inexplicable night, dispersing light, defeating all desire. I have explained to You a hundred times my motives for entering the monastery and You have listened and said nothing, and I have turned away and wept with shame . . .
>
> Lord, God, the whole world tonight seems to be made out of paper. The most substantial things are ready to crumble or tear apart and blow away . . . [6]

God is gift. He cannot be commanded. Up there in that alpine cabin one morning, there came a tearful and profound moment. Kneeling on the wooden floor I told God I would no longer treat him as if I owned him. Life was for him to give and for him to take away. The only claim we have upon him is his love. I confessed the possessiveness that I called 'love for God'. I confessed my attempts to control and dominate. I 'let him go'. I asked for the life that was his gift alone. Something died that day – and something was born. Quietly and surely, spring broke through the death of winter.

For reflection

Have there been times when silence has felt like death to you? Or times when it was full of life? You may like to write them down and reflect on them in the light of this chapter.

Have you ever thought about your death? Perhaps you have experienced the death of a loved one. What thoughts or memories did this chapter provoke in you? Would it help to share them with a friend or in a group? – or tell God about them?

Using an actual cross or crucifix (or a picture of one), spend time silently reflecting upon the death of Christ. What does it mean to you? Are there ways you wished it would mean more?

The Methodist Covenant prayer expresses the letting go and surrendering that we have been exploring. Reflect upon it quietly. If it is appropriate to you, pray it now as an expression of your own self offering.

> I am no longer my own, but yours.
> Put me to what you will, rank me with whom you will;
> Put me to doing, put me to suffering;
> Let me be employed for you or laid aside for you, exalted for you or brought low for you;
> Let me be full, let me be empty;
> Let me have all things, let me have nothing;
> I freely and wholeheartedly yield all things to your pleasure and disposal.
> And now glorious and blessed God, Father, Son and Holy Spirit, you are mine and I am yours.
> So be it.
> And the covenant made on earth,
> Let it be ratified in heaven.
> Amen.

SEVEN

STUFFED OWLS AND WAITING ROOMS

Take nothing for the journey.

Luke 9:3

Blessed are the simple, for they shall have much peace.

Thomas à Kempis

I wait for the Lord,
my soul waits, and in his word I put my hope.
My soul waits for the Lord,
more than watchmen for the morning

Ps.130:6

The desert teaches us four main lessons about praying and believing. The desert is a place of simplicity and waiting, of struggle and adoration. It is these themes we will explore in the next two chapters.[1]

Simplicity

When I joined a study programme in the Middle East a few years ago it included a journey in the Sinai wilderness. I was sent a special kit list for this field trip. Plenty of sun-blocking cream, a wide-brimmed hat (and string to tie it on), strong boots, a sweater for the cold nights, light hard-wearing clothes for the day, and a large water-container. It was stressed in bold type that there was no space for anything else. In the desert you carry only what is necessary. For severely practical reasons, the desert is not a place for luxuries or comforts.

It reminded me of a scene in the film *Lawrence of Arabia*. While on a long exhausting night journey across the desert, a soldier was so tired that he fell off his camel as he slept and didn't wake until the dawn. None of the men with him heard his fall in the night, and in the morning he found himself alone in the vast empty desert. He began to walk. As the sun got hotter he felt the weight of his guns and ammunition and threw them to the sand one by one. Next his dagger, belt and cloak. Within a matter of hours, under the burning sun, this strong warrior was reduced to a shuffling crawl, mercilessly stripped to nothing. He collapsed on the desert floor helplessly waiting death – or rescue.

The desert ruthlessly exposes us to what is essential to life and survival. It is a hard teacher. These are lessons of life and death. There is no margin for error, no respect for reputation or human strength. It was this same wilderness that shaped and matured the life of God's people. There they learned their absolute dependence upon God.

STUFFED OWLS

It is often a crisis in life that exposes us to the emptiness of our securities or lifestyle. The most prized possessions and achievements can become empty of meaning with the loss of a loved one, for example. During the Indian uprising at the end of the last century, British army families had to evacuate in a great hurry. It was reported that the roads in the area were littered with stuffed owls and other bits of Victorian bric-a-brac – the kind of articles you 'wouldn't dream of parting with'. Now, all of a sudden these 'necessities' seemed very unimportant.

Simplicity is a gift. It is something to be discovered both in our inner world and in our outward living. Spiritually and materially, it is a practical necessity. In a world of massive injustices and inequality, it is also a Christian responsibility. One of the urgent demands facing our rampant consumer society in the West today is to learn to share the resources of the world. And for those of us in the West, who dominate the world markets, that means being willing to learn how light we can travel. We are so familiar with our relative wealth and choices and possessions that we take them for granted. We confuse necessities with luxuries. Our worlds are cluttered with stuffed owls.

By uncomfortable coincidence, I found myself moving home last year at the same time as the television screens were filled with pictures of famine victims and refugees in the Sudan. I pride myself on having few possessions. But as I sat surrounded by my boxes and tea chests I watched a family of refugees arriving at a relief camp. They walked in silence, thin and drawn, carrying two small plastic bags. They too were moving home.

SIMPLICITY OF HEART

Simplicity has its source in a quality of heart. Having no possessions does not guarantee a life free from

73

the compulsions of our appetites and greed. Likewise, persons entrusted with great wealth and material goods may yet live in the freedom of simplicity, unpossessed by their possessions. It is an inner freedom that has to be learned. In the introduction to his journal, *The Genesee Diary*, Henri Nouwen tells what led him to break away from his busy ministry to enter the silence of a monastery for six months:

> I realised that I was caught in a web of strange paradoxes. While complaining about too many demands, I felt uneasy when none were made. While speaking about the burden of letter writing, an empty mailbox made me sad. While fretting about tiring lecture tours, I felt disappointed when there were no invitations. While speaking nostalgically about an empty desk, I feared the day in which that would come true. In short, while desiring to be alone I was frightened of being left alone. The more I became aware of these paradoxes, the more I started to see how much I had fallen in love with my own compulsions and illusions, and how much I needed to step back and wonder, 'Is there a quiet stream underneath the fluctuating affirmations and rejections of my little world? Is there a still point where my life is anchored and from which I can reach out with hope and courage and confidence?'[2]

In his book he goes on to record his journey into the simplicity of silence and the pain of 'letting go'. Rather than 'doing' something about his busy-ness – he did precisely the opposite. He stopped and 'did' nothing. Silence has a way of revealing our compulsions and then loosening our grip on them. Someone once described the action of silence as like a glue solvent. It dissolves things that have got stuck together to leave us free to take fresh hold on what really matters. That was Henri Nouwen's experience during his time in silence. As we noted earlier, we seek outer silence in order to learn inner silence. Keeping a 'little desert in the heart', a still centre, is the beginning of simplicity in a complex world.

THE FREEDOM OF SIMPLICITY

This is why I went to the cabin in the Swiss Alps for two months. There my time was my own and I could choose to spend it how I liked. I had a simple daily structure of prayer, Bible reading, study and some manual work. But day by day I still encountered all the compulsions that had begun to grip and exhaust my life with such wearying complexity. I found I could not read my Bible without starting to write a sermon about it in my mind. I could not read any book without 'looking for useful illustrations' for talks. Here I was alone on top of a mountain and still compulsively living as if I had an audience in front of me!

I also found it very hard just to sit and be still without a real anxiety that I had to justify what I was doing. But there was no one to justify myself to. Sometimes in the wide empty spaces of that solitude I experienced real fear that what I was doing was all terribly wrong. Completely alone in the alpine cabin I could be worrying what people were thinking about me. I rehearsed ways of explaining my solitude in ways that sounded profound and 'spiritual'. The truth was that these were the anxieties and compulsions that had been driving me through life. Now, in the silence, they were revealed for what they were. I experienced their power – and their absurdity. I could begin to let them go.

Until we find a place to stop and face these pressures and fears for what they are, we go through life like herded cattle. We are constantly pulled into a complex round of activities designed to make us feel useful, secure and loved. The simple truth is this. We have been selling ourselves on some kind of social and emotional consumer market. And no one dares stop and challenge this in case the 'market' collapses and we are left with nothing but the bitter truth of our real poverty.

Inner simplicity, a nakedness of spirit before God, learned in the desert of loving silence, must lead to outer simplicity. One of the questions that most betrays our complacency is the issue of suffering in the world. Why does God allow the poor to starve and suffer? The real question to ask is much nearer home – why does God allow the rich not to share? In his book *Celebration of Discipline*, Richard Foster makes some helpful suggestions to assist the nurturing of outer simplicity.[3] His ideas include buying things for their practical value rather than status, avoiding things that create an addiction or compulsion, developing the habit of giving things away, learning to enjoy things without possessing them, being sceptical of 'labour-saving devices' and credit availability, and learning to say simply 'yes' or 'no' in response to things. This is all very close to the requirements of life in the desert. There it is understood that to clutter your life can mean death. You must be free to move in the desert. Simplicity is freedom.

Waiting

One feature of travelling through desert lands is the amount of waiting involved. Nothing hurries – and the attitude is that nothing *should* hurry. It is not laziness or the heat or inefficiency. It is an attitude to life that has much to teach us. Waiting is not an interruption to a journey. It is an essential part of the journey itself. In our modern world we have no positive use for waiting. Vast amounts of research goes into doing things quicker and more 'efficiently'. Waiting has become a complete inconvenience, an intrusion. It delays us. It wastes our precious time. John Fowles makes a fascinating comment on the modern attitude to time in *The French Lieutenant's Woman*, comparing it with the experience of Charles, a Victorian gentleman:

Though Charles liked to think of himself as a scientific young man and would probably not have been too surprised had news reached him out of the future of the aeroplane, the jet engine, television, radar; what *would* have astounded him was the changed attitude to time itself. The supposed great misery of our century is the lack of time; our sense of that is why we devote such a huge proportion of our ingenuity and income of our societies to finding faster ways of doing things – as if the final aim of mankind was to grow closer not to a perfect humanity, but to a perfect lightning flash. But for Charles, and for almost all his contemporaries and social peers, the time signature over existence was firmly *adagio*. The problem was not fitting in all that one wanted to do, but spinning out what one did to occupy the vast colonnades of leisure available.[4]

Having to wait involves a submission. We cannot force the bus to arrive any sooner or the doctor's waiting room to empty faster. But our fury over a train delay or even petty disruptions to our timetable shows how hard we find it to live with the truth of this. Waiting is an acknowledgement of our dependency. It exposes to us the illusion of our 'control' over our lives. So it is in Christian prayer. The God of the Bible is the God of the desert. He *walks* with his people. He is the 'Three-mile-an-hour God'. One of the most frustrating but essential lessons of Christian prayer is that God is not to be hurried. We are learning a new pace of life and new priorities to live by.

How deflating it is when, full of love and zeal, we decide to 'wait upon the Lord'. After some worship and prayer, full of faith and confidence, we find ourselves sitting in silence – waiting. Nothing happens. And there is nothing we can do about it. It is so irritating having to wait for someone when you have taken the trouble to get ready in good time! In the desert of the Spirit we wait because we have to. Our life depends upon the arrival of the living God. But in the Bible that is not a negative dependency at all. In fact waiting for God is something very positive. Nor is it an idle or passive sitting around. Waiting is an activity. In Psalm 123, we have the image of waiting at the table of the master or mistress. 'As the eyes of the slaves look to the hand of their master . . . so our eyes look to the Lord our

78

God' (123:2,3). Waiting is then a place of faithful obedience, ready to respond and serve the moment the need arises. It is attentive and full of concentration on the will of the master.

Another image of waiting is expressed by the watchfulness of the guards on the walls of a city (see Isaiah 21:8). They guard the city against evil. Waiting here is a determined vigilance against danger. Jesus himself taught his disciples to have the same vigilance: 'Watch and pray so that you will not fall into temptation' (Mark 14:38).

TESTING OUR DESIRE

But the waiting is also something full of hope and vision. The guards on the wall not only look for danger – they also watch for the first joyful sight of the King returning to the city. 'I wait for the Lord, . . . and in his word I put my hope. My soul waits for the Lord more than watchmen for the morning' (Ps.130:6). Jesus used the picture of keeping awake while waiting for the bridegroom to arrive to start a wedding celebration (Matt. 25:6). In fact waiting and hoping are the same thing in the Bible. 'They that wait upon the Lord shall renew their strength', in Isaiah's famous prophecy (40:31) is also translated, 'They that *hope* in the Lord . . .' Once again, the picture of waiting is active and demanding, but something alive and eager.

So waiting also expresses love and longing. The psalmist thirsts for God like a desert waiting for rain (Ps.63:1). Waiting sharpens desire. In fact it helps us to recognise where our real desires lie. It separates our passing enthusiasms from our true longings.

It reveals to us both our shallowness and our depths. Waiting is a test of our love and longing.

THE FOOLISHNESS OF WAITING

On the headland overlooking the bay of the Lee Abbey estate is the old Duty Point tower. From that small stone tower the view is breathtaking. You can follow the rugged cliff coast for some distance in the both directions, and directly across the Bristol Channel is the South Wales coastline. No ship or sailing boat can pass unseen from there. Above and around it the gulls wheel and cry around the seasons of the years. That tower always speaks to me of vigilance and waiting. I used to spend time there in all weathers and all seasons. It could be a place of glorious vision at dawn or sunset. It could be a place of wild battering and frightening exposure. All the storms struck there first as they rolled inland off the sea. From the bitter cold of winter to the high summer heat, that simple, solitary tower, high up on the headland, came to express every mood of Christian hope and longing for God.

The first time I noticed it I asked what it was. I was told it was a 'folly'. Well, we have much to learn from such foolishness.

THE ORDINARINESS OF WAITING

'Lord give me patience – NOW!'
There is no quick way to learn patience unfortunately. And there is nothing romantic about learning simplicity and waiting. It is tough. It involves an emptying. It means a space must be cleared in the midst of the clutter of our lives. And there we must sit and be still and wait for God in hope and pati-

80

ence. It will feel rather useless or a 'waste of time'. But it is actually challenging our whole understanding of what is useful. This quiet, unhurried work of the Spirit begins when we give space for God at the heart of our lives. It is a silence of humble submission. In the clutter and complexity of the modern world, it is the only reliable preparation for following Christ. Anything else would be easier in some ways. If only we could claim we were in the depths of 'the dark night of the soul', or some great process of breaking, suffering and remaking! But it is really very ordinary, dry and tedious. As Thomas Merton writes, 'We need to be emptied. Otherwise prayer is only a game. And yet it is pride to want to be stripped and humbled in the grand manner with thunder and lightning. The simplest and most effective way to sanctity is to disappear into the background of ordinary everyday routine.'[5]

For reflection

What thoughts came to mind as you read this chapter?

SIMPLICITY

Consider Richard Foster's suggestions on nurturing simplicity (page 76). Are there practical responses you can make in considering simplicity? One idea might be to walk silently through your home. Notice your belongings and all the things that make up your life. Where do you keep your 'stuffed owls'?

Thank God for all that you have. Be aware of your frustrations and longings for what you do not have. Offer to God all that makes up your life at this time and pray for a simplicity of heart to guide your living.

WAITING

When was the last time you were kept waiting? What were your feelings about it? Are there things that God is keeping you waiting about at this moment? What is that teaching you? Taking the four pictures of waiting for God mentioned above (attentiveness, vigilance, hope and love), compose your own prayer to God using each of those images.

EIGHT

DUST AND GLORY

At once, the Spirit sent him out into the desert.

Mark 1:12

Is my gloom, after all,
Shade of his hand, outstretched caressingly?

Francis Thompson

O how I fear thee living God,
with deepest, tenderest fears . . .

William Faber

The desert and the parched land will be glad;
   the wilderness will rejoice and blossom . . .
they will see the glory of the Lord,
   the splendour of our God . . .

Isa. 35:1-2

Simplicity and waiting are only learned through testing and therefore through struggle. Struggle is, in
fact, one of the signs we are growing as Christians.
Christian prayer is marked more often by struggle
than by peace. But unless we understand this, we
will have no way of understanding the times of dryness and darkness that come to us all.

Struggle

An important insight into Christian struggle comes from what might be considered an unexpected source. In recent decades, many churches and individuals have had their lives excitingly renewed by experiencing the power of the Holy Spirit in a fresh way. The Charismatic Renewal has made a profound impact on the churches of this country and has led many into a wonderful release of worship and prayer. God has become gloriously real. But those involved in leadership and pastoral care within the Charismatic movement found themselves regularly trying to guide people for whom the experience had gone dry. It was not that the initial experience of the Spirit was unreal. Nor had they been particularly misled. What was needed in the church was a Christian understanding of the wilderness.

When Jesus was baptised in the Jordan and filled with the Spirit, Mark's gospel actually says he was 'driven' into the wilderness by the Spirit. Clearly for Jesus, it wasn't just life in the world that was testing and struggle – it was life in the Spirit! John Richards, in a booklet on this theme, suggests that these times of dryness and struggle are not a negative denial of blessing but a 'positive preparation for ministry' – as they were for Christ himself. He goes on to say, 'there is no better summary of the wilderness experience than that well known chorus,

> Spirit of the living God
> Fall afresh on me. . . .
> break me, melt me, mould me, fill me . . .' [1]

This is an important discovery to make in our Christian lives. Not all dryness, struggle and darkness is 'wrong' or negative. And through all such times we may learn to follow the life of Christ more closely. In fact, in the real deserts of the world, people do all their serious travelling by night, guided by the stars. The light and heat of the day makes safe journeying impossible. That may be a helpful picture of darkness in the Christian life. Of course, not all darkness is good, but many of us have yet to discover the reverse – that not all darkness is bad. Unless we accept this, there is a danger that our worship and prayer may be a desperate clinging to the light because we are afraid of the dark. Darkness is assumed to be a defeat and failure.

There is nothing sadder than a Christian fellowship where every song must be of victory, every prayer full of faith, every member always smiling and joyful. It is an exhausting pretence to keep up for long, and it condemns those who cannot hide from their fears to further pain of failure and inadequacy. It is actually dishonest. It means that we can never offer our tears as well as our smiles, our questions as well as our certainties, our wounds as well as our victories. It means that we are always keeping Christ out of the very places in our lives where we need him most – the place of our darkness, uncertainties and fears. It also means in practice that we will keep talking and chattering to avoid silence. As we have already seen, silence has a way of insisting upon truth.

In the night of faith

In the light of this, how are we to understand and respond to the times of dryness and darkness that meet us in our lives? In making the following suggestions I wish to acknowledge the help of Philip Seddon's booklet *Darkness*.[2] It has been for me one of the most original and profound reflections on this important area of Christian experience.

DARKNESS OF SEPARATION

The Bible is clear that sin separates us from God. In the darkness of the cross, Jesus himself entered the terrible darkness of that separation with his aweful cry, 'My God, why have you forsaken me?' (Mark 15:34). Christ has journeyed deeply into the darkness of this world, into all its places of separation and loss. But this does not mean that we escape it. Rather, it means that we are not alone in the dark and are protected from its deepest threat to us. Through him we can find the courage to face our own sin and separation.

In moments when our own hearts are dark and troubled we could begin by examining our hearts. One way to do this is by sitting or kneeling silently and asking the Holy Spirit to bring to awareness anything that might 'shed light' on our darkness. If there is sin or wrong-doing there we need to confess it, change our behaviour and ask that God's forgiveness would restore us to the light. But the truth is that we both sin, and we are sinned against. Sometimes the darkness may not be our own. The help of an experienced friend or pastor may be important, silently waiting upon God together, asking for dis-

cernment and guidance. This is especially true where
there is a possibility that the darkness has its source
in evil of any kind.

Our darkness may be due to a loss of familiar securities. It may be caused by a crisis at work or at home,
or it may have a more hidden root. But it is the
work of the Holy Spirit to shake us from other securities until we trust in God alone. This may be what
happens when people find that worship that was
previously exciting and uplifting suddenly goes dead
and empties of meaning for them. This is very distressing, especially when everyone around you is still
full of life and joy. But our security can never be in
a particular style of worship or 'experience' of God;
it must be in God alone. George Appleton wrote a
prayer that expresses this well:

> O Christ, my Lord, again and again I have said
> with Mary Magdalene, 'They have taken away my
> Lord and I know not where they have laid him.'
> I have been desolate and alone. And thou hast
> found me again, and I know that what has died is
> not thou, my Lord, but only my idea of thee, the
> image I have made to preserve what I have found
> and to be my security. I shall make another image,
> O Lord, better than the last. That too must go,
> and all successive images, until I come to the
> blessed vision of thyself, O Christ, my Lord.[3]

At such times of darkness, we have to give ourselves
to God by faith and not by sight. Light and darkness
are the same to God (Ps. 139:12). Our silence can

express our submission to this 'severe mercy' in God's love.

THE SHADOW OF GOD

'Is my gloom, after all, Shade of his hand, out-stretched caressingly?'[4] asked Francis Thompson. A favourite picture of security in the Bible is of a young bird overshadowed by its parent's wings. In Psalm 63, a man in a painful desert of faith encourages himself by remembering the past goodness of God. His darkness then takes on a new significance: 'Then I sing for joy in the shadow of your wings' (63:7). Sometimes the shadow is that of a rock holding off a wind or storm for us. The hymn, 'Rock of Ages', was inspired by such an experience.

The truth is that the closer we are to someone the less we see of them. Presence becomes more important than sight. Consider a mountain. We see it clearly ahead of us and decide to climb it. But when we start to climb we lose sight of it. It is too close to see. In such a sense darkness may be the presence not the absence of God. We press on, growing into a deeper trust and love, by faith, not by sight.

DAZZLING DARKNESS

From the teachings of the saints of the Orthodox Church comes the idea that some darkness is not the lack of light, but the excess of it. This is called the 'Apophatic' tradition. It is sometimes translated the 'Negative Way', but that gives a misleading impression in English. Rather like the blindness that strikes us when we look directly at the sun, the vision of God blinds us. It really isn't surprising that in

88

drawing near to the glory of God our normal sense of sight and sound and touch should prove inadequate. God is literally unseen. So to draw near him means entering a place beyond sight and mind. This is darkness and mystery, and so the place of 'finding' God is also experienced initially as bewildering loss.

For St John of the Cross, night and darkness may be the friends, not the enemies of faith. He taught that God leads us into a 'night' in which our senses – our usual ways of feeling and experiencing life – are emptied. There follows a deep darkness of purifying and waiting, that ultimately leads to the dawn, the vision of God, deepened and enriched. He stressed that all this was under the leading of the Spirit and cannot be manufactured. While travelling through this night of faith, the Christian needs careful and discerning guidance. It is never a journey that we are asked to take without guidance and support. And the final intention of this darkness is that we should fall through it into divine love. 'Oh night that guided me, Oh night, more lovely than the dawn, Oh night that joined the Beloved with lover, transformed in the Beloved!'[5]

This is obviously a part of Christian experience and journey that needs mature understanding. Church congregations need wise pastors and guides who are experienced in the ways of the Spirit. In fact the theme of this whole book is one which belongs in the context of the life and discipline of the Christian fellowship. Silence and solitude need the discipline, support and nourishment of shared Christian life, Bible reading and Holy Communion. They cannot be an alternative to it.

Adoration

The desert is supremely a place of worship and adoration. The tough lessons of desert faith are all to bring us to the place of glorious communion with the living God. Indeed the promise of God's salvation and re-creation does not come to cities or to any of the places of human achievement and accomplishment. It is promised to the deserts and waste places. It is the desert that waits in hope for the salvation of God. It is there that we are called to prepare for his coming (Isa. 40:3).

> The desert and the parched land wili be glad,
>   the wilderness will rejoice and blossom.
> Like a crocus, it will burst into bloom;
>   it will rejoice greatly and shout for joy.
> The glory of Lebanon will be given to it,
>   the splendour of Carmel and Sharon;
> they will see the glory of the Lord,
>   the splendour of our God . . .   (Isa. 35:1–3)

THE COMPANIONSHIP OF CREATION

The awareness of the participation of creation in the worship of God is a regular feature of the Scriptures. It frequently occurs in the poetry of the psalms where mountains, seas, trees, animals and birds are all joining in the praise of God. In Psalm 19, creation is pouring out a torrent of praise, night and day, never heard, but 'their voice goes out into all the earth' (19:4). In Romans, chapter 8, creation is waiting eagerly for the fulfilling of God's salvation among the human race – and thus to all the world. The participation of all creation in the worship and longing for God has been a neglected area of Christian understanding. There is nothing sentimental about it. Just as the psalmist drew glorious inspiration from creation around him, so can we. One personal experience of this may illustrate the importance of this truth.

During my time of alpine solitude there were moments of light and darkness, of joy and pain. On one particular day my praying led me into a place of pain and darkness. I spent a long while weeping without really understanding the meaning of my tears. I finally got up and began to prepare an evening meal. I was not very hungry but finished the meal, and as was my practice, I read the gospel passage set for the day. The first words were 'You did not choose me, but I chose you' (John 15:16). The words were suddenly very awesome and overwhelming, and I began again to weep, feeling very lost and a little frightened in the mystery of it all. After a while the tears stopped and I became still with a mixture of numbness and heightened awareness that can often follow an outpouring of grief. I became aware of my small log stove behind me. There in the corner of the room it crackled and clunked while the leaky old kettle on top hissed and steamed. It had the feel of a wise old friend who loved and understood but would not intrude upon this moment by coming nearer. I became aware of the cabin around me. The bare plank walls of my cabin felt supporting, secure and sheltering – but without closing in upon my space. I lifted my head and looked out of the window. I watched the pasture grasses blowing in the evening wind, the clouds on the mountain tops and felt the cooling air of the approaching night. Everything around me seemed

to understand. I was filled with a deep reverence
and awe for creation. And I knew that at the heart
of that moment I had received the presence of God
in a quite new way. From a place of struggle, darkness and desolation, had come resurrection and
worship.

LOVE'S REWARD

But worship is not yet adoration; much worship
stops short of adoration. We worship and thank God
for what he does. Adoration begins when we are
captivated by *who he is*. Adoration is not appreci-
ation but abandonment. There must come a point
where all discussion, talking and understanding, run
out, 'lost in wonder, love and praise'. That is the
heart of desert faith – kneeling in the silence of
eternity to have kindled within us the holy flame of
adoration and love. We all need a particular point
of focus to lead us into adoration. It may the contemplation of a verse of Scripture, or gazing upon a
cross. For the Desert Fathers the supreme focus
for the adoration of God was the Eucharist. To
contemplate in the bread and wine, the gift of Christ,
was to contemplate the heart of God's mercy, love
and unimaginable glory. It was to bow in the shadow
of his awe-ful holiness.

O, how I fear thee, living God,
With deepest, tenderest fears,
And worship thee with trembling hope,
And penitential tears.

Father of Jesus, love's reward,
What rapture will it be,

Prostrate before thy throne to lie,
And gaze, and gaze on thee.[6]

For reflection

STRUGGLE

Dietrich Bonhoeffer wrote 'to be simple is to fix
one's eyes solely on the simple truth of God at a
time when all concepts are being confused, distorted
and turned upside down'.[7]

There are times when the struggle and turmoil of
life makes stillness almost impossible. At times like
that it can be helpful to pray the Jesus prayer (see
page 12). It acts rather like a lead on a dog who
can't help wandering off, distracted by everything
around it. Each refrain of the prayer pulls us back
to our focus on God.

In what areas of your life do you find it hardest to
trust God? In times of darkness and dryness, the
psalmist often deliberately recalls moments when
God's goodness has been real and present. This is
not to cling to past experiences, but to strengthen
faith and trust while it is hard at the present time.

Are there such times you can look back on to strengthen your faith and hope in dark times? It may help
to write them down.

ADORATION

Have you ever prayed and worshipped with creation,
as the psalmist does? You could write a psalm

including the glory (or tangles) of your garden or street, or a nearby park.

How do you prepare to receive communion? It may be possible before or after a communion service to spend time focusing on what you are receiving. In your own home you could perhaps use a piece of bread and some wine as a visual aid.

Pray for a glorious abandonment into God's love, for the fire of his presence to burn at the heart of your being.

PART III

IN THE MIDST OF LIFE

NINE

THE LANGUAGE OF
THE MAD

No man can control the tongue . . . out of the same
mouth comes praise and cursing.

Jas. 3:8–9

Let your 'Yes' be 'Yes', and your 'No', 'No'.

Matt. 5:37

I felt as if I had touched something that should not
be touched, as if I had distorted something simply
by talking about it, as if I had tried to touch a dew
drop.

Henri Nouwen

Do not let your mouth lead you into sin . . . many
words are meaningless. Therefore stand in the awe
of God.

Eccles. 5:6–7

When we are silent we are not giving up on words.
We are silent around the words we speak, out of
respect for their truth and power. We are silent
because we love words too much to see them abused.
Earlier in this book we spoke of the way that
silence and solitude give a kind of punctuation to
our lives. Silence and solitude give balance and

meaning to the script of our lives. This is particularly true in our relationship with the words we speak. James sees the tongue as something we must learn to tame. Like the small rudder that steers a large and powerful ship, the tongue

> . . . is a small part of the body, but it makes great boasts. Consider what a great forest is set on fire by a small spark. The tongue is also a fire, a world of evil among the parts of the body. It corrupts the whole person, sets the whole course of his life on fire, and is itself set on fire by hell. . . . No man can control the tongue . . . out of the same mouth comes praise and cursing.   (Jas. 3:5–8)

War of words

Does that sound pessimistic? In this age of mass media words are actually more powerful than ever. International peace treaties or nuclear arms negotiations can break down for lack of the right 'form of words' that all parties can sign in agreement. Industrial conflicts often become a 'war of words'. Whole disputes may arise from one careless or ill-judged remark by one side or another. Words unite and words divide. Words reveal and words distort. In the summer of 1989 the world watched the rise of the pro-democracy movement in China. The Chinese government brutally repressed it. But more horrifying was the propaganda that followed. The authorities cynically rewrote and reinterpreted the events themselves. Good was called bad, peace was called violence. For good or ill, those who control words and their communication have enormous power in shaping what people believe and understand.

In Morris West's novel *Proteus* the Russian Ambassador is being questioned by a personal friend about the state of the world:

> 'What is the thing you are most afraid of?'
> 'Politically or personally?'
> 'Both.'
> 'It is a thing which has happened already, whose human consequences are already upon us. We have so debased human language that it is impossible to believe any longer what we hear or read. I tell you "yes", the echo answers "no". We state one position and negotiate another. You talk "food", I hear "bombs". We have created a language of the mad. You show on television bodies broken in a railway accident. The next instant some impossibly beautiful wench is demonstrating how to make floors shine like glass. The illusion is complete. There are no bodies. There could never be blood on so bright a surface.'[1]

What the Ambassador was worried about is our cynical capacity to distort reality to make it more bearable. When the atom bomb was dropped on Hiroshima, President Truman was informed by the code phrase, 'Baby delivered on time'. Current research into the effect of Strontium 90 radio-active fall-out is called 'Project Sunshine'. Only public protest stopped the US navy naming a nuclear submarine 'Corpus Christi' (the Body of Christ) a few years ago. We live in a world that has learned to use words to cover up what is really going on. We use words for propaganda purposes. The warning of Isaiah the prophet is as timely as ever: 'Woe to those who call evil good and good evil, who put darkness for light and light for darkness, who put bitter for sweet and sweet for bitter' (5:20).

Caring for words

But we all use words to our own ends. It is not just politicians and governments that have a 'way with words'. It is a temptation we all face. That is why Jesus taught his disciples to keep a simple directness and honesty of speech. Do not reinforce your words with promises and oaths, he said: 'Let your "Yes" be "Yes", and your "No", "No"; anything beyond this comes from the evil one' (Matt. 5:37). Once language loses that simplicity and truth it becomes emptied of meaning, and no amount of reinforcement by promises or vows will restore trust. As the proverb says, 'When words are many, sin is not absent, but he who holds his tongue is wise' (Prov. 10:19).

As Christians we are not just responsible for the words we speak. We have a concern for the truth of words wherever they are used – for the words by which the world is living. The discipline of silence brings us into a new relationship with words and how we are using them. Silence has a way of testing us and restoring truth and life to the words we use. It also exposes the shallowness of our words and the duplicity of the motives behind them. This understanding led Thomas Merton to describe prayer as 'the unmasking of illusion'.

During his extended period in a monastery Henri Nouwen noticed the way that silence was making him more sensitive to words. After one conversation he experienced remorse and guilt: 'I felt as if I had touched something that should not be touched, as if I had distorted something simply by talking about it, as if I had tried to grasp a dew drop.'[2]

During my own time of silence in the alpine cabin I experienced what felt like a complete collapse of language. It was as if I had been making words work so hard that now in the silence they fell away from my control, exhausted and emptied of meaning. And that was close to the truth. It was a disturbing experience, because I had always been someone with an ability to use words. Now all of a sudden I could find no words to express myself with or pray with. What replaced them was tears. Nothing had prepared me for the amount of weeping I would do in the solitude of my cabin. Tears replaced language for me. I wept for joy, I wept for sorrow. I wept in pain or beauty, in worship or in penitence.

As time went by I found words returning and I began to understand the experience of Henri Nouwen. I too wanted to use words much more carefully. I took new delight in words and played with them, delighting in their sounds and subtlety of meaning. Words became fuller and richer in meaning, and often one word was more than enough to express a whole prayer or thought. I delighted in the way that God speaks his 'Word'. One word – Christ – says it all. No word can be fuller and richer in meaning.

Through it all I became aware of the extraordinary way we waste the gift of words. We use them to protect our insecurities and we cast them carelessly around our every encounter. Twisted and emptied of meaning, we litter our lives with them. Then, when we really need words to communicate, to love and to understand, we wonder that they are so hard to find.

From the Celtic Christians of the Scottish Isles comes a moving example of the reverencing of words. These simple rural folk had prayers, blessings and songs for every part of life. For centuries these 'runes' have been passed on from generation to generation, as familiar and important to them as the soil they tilled and the seas they farmed. In the last century, Alexander Carmichael spent years collecting them into a book. A crofter shared with him a very beautiful going-to-sleep rune one evening. The next morning the man walked twenty-six miles to see Carmichael and make him promise not to publish his 'little prayer'. 'Think ye', said the old man, 'if I slept a wink last night for thinking of what I had given away. Proud, indeed, shall I be, if it give pleasure to yourself, but I should not like cold eyes to read it in a book.'[3]

But it is not just eyes that can be cold. Lips and hearts can be cold as well, if words do not live for us in the richness of their given sense. That loving reverence for a well used prayer contrasts so starkly with the ease of spontaneous prayer that characterises some Christian worship today.

Speaking by silence

In some parts of the world people are much more careful with silence than we are. They know it is an important and powerful part of the way we communicate with each other. European culture has always used words to establish relationships. Many

Asian and African cultures have always understood the power of 'presence' between people. So an English person meeting someone says, 'Pleased to meet you, how are you?' An African will say, 'I see you.'

Mahatma Gandhi is a fascinating example of this approach to people. In the midst of a turbulent political campaign we find him offering silence to his followers. Louis Fischer tells us that:

> . . . sometimes, if he was too tired or the crowd too noisy, he would sit on the platform in silence until the crowd, which often numbered two hundred thousand, became quiet. He then continued to sit in silence, and the men and women sat in silence, and he touched his palms together to bless them, and smiled and departed. This was communication without words, and the mass silence was an exercise in self-control, and self-searching, a step therefore towards self-rule.[4]

Silence has always been a way of protesting. Recent campaigns for abortion law reform and nuclear disarmament have included marches of silent witness. If you have ever stood in such a crowd you will have experienced the persuasive power of silence. So it is not surprising to find that the most active protesters in the Church are the silent Quakers. On issues of social and political injustice they are always awake and active. Their silence leads them into protest and action.

Silence sifts and judges us. It gives a new awareness. So it will always have that edge of protest about it. And in the end the only words to speak are those that lead to peace and truth in the gospel of Christ. The silence of Christian faith and prayer is rooted in our understanding of God and the mystery of his presence. St Ignatius, an important leader in the early Church, taught that silence can point people to God more than our words. In particular he looked for a quality of silence in all leaders of the Church:

> A bishop should be particularly revered when he is silent. The silence of a bishop bears witness to the reality of God, both in the mystery of his divine silence and in the silence of his passion. The church is the place where all things pass over into reality by being plunged into the hidden reality of God, so the outer and inner become one, the word and silence are reunited.[5]

It is not true that by keeping silent we are saying nothing. Silence can express all kinds of moods and feelings. And of course there are times when we should be speaking and refuse to be silent. We can sin by silence. But Ignatius is speaking of a positive silence out of reverence for God's presence and the mystery of his will. It is an absurd anxiety for a church leader to feel that he or she must have something to say on every occasion. God alone has such knowledge. All our talking and discussing may satisfy our need to be 'doing something', but it will not lead us or the world any deeper into insight or God's presence. The most we will achieve is to set up a few more committees. By staying silent, Ignatius says, we bear witness to the deeper realities that we, and our world, need reminding of. Above all, we bear witness to the priority of God and his purposes. So, says the philosopher in Ecclesiastes,

Do not be quick with your mouth,
  do not be hasty in your heart
  to utter anything before God.
God is in heaven
  and you are on earth,
  so let your words be few . . .
Do not let your mouth lead you into sin . . .
  many words are meaningless.
Therefore stand in awe of God.   (Eccles. 5:2–7)

Guarding the tongue

While on the subject of language and words it is
important to consider the gift of tongues. To anyone
encountering it for the first time this gift could
equally be called the language of the mad! But this
gift of prayer and worship has been a significant
expression of the Christian renewal movement this
century. I want to say that when I write urging Christians to explore silence in prayer I am not denying
this gift. I have used it myself for a number of years.
The whole burden of this chapter is not a rejection
of language and words but a deeper reverence in the
use of them.

Many people using the gift of tongues seem to
follow an unwritten rule that tongues must be
spoken extremely fast. I am not sure why this is so,
but one result is that worship is more cluttered with
words than ever – of whatever language. It is possible, and surely more natural, to speak or pray in
tongues at the same speed as any other language. In
my own experience a word or phrase in tongues, as
with English, may be all that is needed at times of

worship or silent prayer. The disciplining of the tongue applies as much to tongues as to English.

Neither is tongues an escape from facing hard questions and reflection. We must be willing to have such a gift tested in the searching silence of God. This has not always been allowed to happen in the Church. Thomas Merton noted some particular occasions when the phenomena of tongues appeared in Southern Baptist churches in America in the 1960s. One was during the early civil rights demonstrations, another was during the Cuba crisis and the beginnings of American involvement in Vietnam. He wrote this:

> At a time when the churches were at last becoming uneasily aware of a grave responsibility to *say something* about civil rights and nuclear war, the ones who could be least expected to be articulate on such subjects (and who often had solid dogmatic prejudices that foreclosed all discussion) began to cry out in unknown tongues . . . One thing is quite evident about this phenomenon. He who speaks in an unknown tongue can safely speak without fear of contradiction. His utterance forecloses all dialogue.[6]

It is no new temptation to use religion to hide from hard issues and 'real life'. But neither silence nor tongues are intended to provide any such escape from reality. Rather with all the gifts the Spirit gives, we seek, in the midst of life, 'the hidden reality of God, so the outer and inner become one, the word and silence are reunited'.

For reflection

IN CORPORATE WORSHIP

In the liturgy of the Anglican services there are now many points where 'a silence may be kept'. Many churches ignore these in practice. Word and silence can be brought together in many simple ways. For example, keeping silence after scripture reading or after the sermon. Once the congregation grow accustomed to this it doesn't need announcing.

In times of 'open' prayer and worship, keep time to be silent – this does not mean songs or prayers about being silent! (The leader needs to exercise discipline at this point.) Another place of natural stillness may be after the thanksgiving prayer at communion or after everyone has received communion (the organist may need discipline at this point!).

Incidentally, the presence of children does not automatically preclude silence. Most children learn an awkwardness in silence from adults around them. As a congregation relaxes with silence, children will enter it too (and the inevitable exceptions won't matter quite so much). You don't need silence outside to be silent inside.

PRAYING IN TONGUES OR IN ENGLISH

Try praying with just a few words – perhaps the name of Jesus or a phrase from the Psalms, or a phrase the Spirit gives in tongues. Quietly repeating them, let the phrase or word lead you into silence and out of it, like a refrain. Jesus tell us not to 'pile up words' when we pray (Matt. 6:7) – try using very few.

TEN

THE LEAPING WORD

You will be silent and not able to speak until the day this happens, because you did not believe my words . . .

Luke 1:20

We are living in days which are not exactly calculated to encourage the career of the prophet . . . the main function of the prophet is to 'listen'.

Michael Harper

The word of God is alive and active, sharper than any double-edged sword.

Heb. 4:12

All things were lying in quiet and silence, and night in her swift course was half spent, when the Almighty Word leapt from thy royal throne in heaven.

Wisd. 18:14

That last verse has been used for centuries by the Church as a Christmas antiphon. It has been used to celebrate the birth of Christ, symbolically expressing God's Word of salvation springing into the world.

Interestingly he comes like a leaping word in the silence.

Word into silence

Silence is a bit of a contradiction. After all, God has spoken! We have good news to share. Didn't Jesus command us to tell the world about him? Yet here we are near the end of a whole book commending the importance of keeping quiet.

Zechariah must have felt like this. He was the father of John the Baptist. He was a priest in the Temple at Jerusalem and nearing the end of a long and faithful ministry (Luke 1:5ff). But the private sadness of Zechariah and his wife Elizabeth was that they had no children. After years of hoping and praying they were now too old to be parents. Barrenness in the Bible is an important symbol. It speaks of fruitlessness, failure and humiliation. Even today it is a source of deep distress, but in the days of Zechariah children were an investment for the future. They ensured caring and food in old age and the dignity of a family line continued. Barrenness has always been a sign of profound human helplessness – it is a dead end.

This is not the most promising way to start a story. But it was in that humanly hopeless situation, God chose to act. One evening, standing in the holiest place of the temple, Zechariah is offering incense and praying on behalf of the people. The familiar Jewish liturgy is on his lips; 'May the merciful God enter the holy place and accept with favour the offering of his people.' And God answers that prayer, and the prayer he and Elizabeth have prayed for so many years (Luke 1:13). To the amazement of Zechariah, an angel appears and promises him a son who will be a great prophet in Israel (1:11–20). He will prepare the way for the Messiah.

Not unreasonably, Zechariah asks how this can be possible. But for questioning the word of Gabriel, he is struck deaf and dumb until the day of John's birth. It seems a very harsh judgement on this elderly man. Zechariah's question seems very reasonable in the light of their age. And besides, this prophecy is the one that his people have been longing and praying for for centuries. But the angel puts him straight into silence and solitary confinement.

So beyond all hope, Elizabeth finds new life hidden and alive in her womb. Beyond all belief, Zechariah finds prophecy trapped in his heart. Elizabeth's response is intuitively to *choose* silence. She withdraws into solitude for most of her pregnancy (1:24). Zechariah joins his wife there, but not from choice. Silence and solitude has been imposed on him.

We are not told what those silent months meant to Zechariah, but the day comes when the child is born and the community gathers to celebrate and witness the naming of the baby (1:57ff). Clearly Zechariah has somehow shared the words of the angel with Elizabeth for she insists that his name must be John. This breaks the tradition of naming the son after the father. They ask Zechariah and he writes on a clay tablet, 'John IS his name'. Luke's original words here are very emphatic. There is great force of conviction, and you can sense Zechariah almost snapping the writing stick in his fervour. And at once the Holy Spirit fills him and releases his tongue. After all those silent months he pours the fullness of his heart into a glorious prophecy that the Christian church has used in worship ever since,

> Praise be to the Lord, the God of Israel,
> because he has come and has redeemed his people. . . .
> And you, my child, will be called a prophet of the Most High.
> for you will go on before the Lord to prepare the way for him . . .   (Luke 1:68–79)

Luke then tells us that John himself lived in the solitude of the desert until his ministry began (1:80). The miraculous story of this whole family has been shaped and guided in solitude and silence.

For Zechariah the word of Gabriel became more than just a verbal promise. In the silence the prophecy had become a living part of him. What must have begun as a painful punishment to him turned into a gift. How often and deeply he must have turned over Gabriel's words and prayed for understanding. The silence and solitude taught him to receive and keep the promise in the deepest place of his being. The word became a fire in his bones. It was a faithful but bewildered old man who entered solitude; it was a prophet that emerged.

A time to speak, a time to be silent

Zechariah's experience illustrates the important relationship between words and silence. They serve and strengthen each other. It may also help us to understand why Jesus often urged the disciples to keep quiet about things they had just seen. Some-

111

times this seemed quite impractical, since he often said it after some spectacular revelation or public miracle (see, for example, Luke 5:12–14, 8:49–56 and 9:28–36). Some quite complicated theological speculations have been offered to explain his attitude. But his intention may have been very practical. Unless the disciples took time to reflect on what they had seen and 'take it in', they would lose its significance.

> Where there was a danger of all deeper impressions being scattered and lost through the garrulous repetition of the outward circumstances of the healing, there silence was enjoined, so that there might be an inward brooding over the gracious and wondrous dealings of the Lord.[1]

The word and works of God in our midst are simply too important to be chattered away and lost. We have already noticed how Jesus himself continually withdrew from the surface of life into silence. He also taught his disciples to do the same. It seems to have been a quality that Luke saw also in Mary, for he comments upon it (Luke 2.18–19). This kind of silence does not belong just to a particular mood, emotion or personality type. Silence is the way that we learn to deepen the moment. We take in its truth and digest it. In the same way meditation is often described as like a cow chewing the cud, or a person sucking their favourite sweet. It is not something to be hurried. You keep chewing or sucking until it has yielded all its goodness and flavour. In silence we learn to take God's word and chew it over until its life and message and significance is received deep within. It must become a part of us. It must 'take flesh'. Had Zechariah understood this he might have

chosen to be silent with God's word. But that is a
hard discipline for anyone. Surely there was mercy
in the judgement of the angel.

We live in a world of instant comment, instant
evaluation, instant everything. We need to learn to
wait for things. We must wait in silence and be
slower to speak. Even the encouragement in Christian groups to share 'what the Lord has done for
you today', may be an unhelpful pressure at times.
There is a time to speak and a time to be silent.
There must be times when we are taking in and
digesting what life is bringing to us. If we encourage
each other to speak, we should also recognise and
guard the moments to be silent.

Silence and the leaping word

The reason we are called to silence, willingly or
unwillingly, is to receive God's word. The story of
Zechariah shows us that silence is vitally linked to
prophecy. In the silence of the Spirit and in contemplation the Word of God springs to life. God is the
only source of the life of the world; the bread of this
age will never sustain us (Luke 4:4). In a society
where much is heard of shrinking churches and the
decline of religion, it is important to realise that the
issue facing the Church is not 'survival but prophecy'. The real issue is life not death. A vital gift of
silence is its ability to open our ears, eyes and hearts
again to receive the living word of God. Michael
Harper considers that we are involved in recovering
a lost art.

We are living in days which are not exactly calculated to encourage the career of the prophet. If the main function of an apostle is to go, then the main function of a prophet is to 'listen'. The Church today is notoriously bad at listening and being still and quiet enough to do so. It talks and writes incessantly, but where are the people who know how to retreat from the world and listen to God? We have bred a whole new race who have never learnt the art of listening to the Lord, and passing on his word to others.[2]

Biblical prophecy is not, as popularly supposed, to do with prediction of future events. It is the proclaiming of a heart and will. It is the revealing of the heart and mind of God to the people of God and so to the world. Its practical expression takes many forms. St Paul teaches that there will be some church members who have a particular gift of prophecy. When such people speak, believing they have a message from God, the rest of the church must carefully weigh what is said and decide if it is authentic (1 Cor. 14:29). But it is equally clear that all Christians should seek and listen for God's guiding word in all parts of their lives. And just as Jesus found that everything around him was alive with signs of God and purposes – stones, birds, trees, harvest fields, children, shops, homes and kitchens – so may we. Every bush is burning with God's life if we are given the eye and heart to perceive it.

'Prophecy' may sound a rather daunting term for our attempts to make sense of daily life and hear God speaking in it. A few examples may illustrate the ways this can happen.

Some years ago I was part of a weekly fellowship group. We met on Wednesday evenings for Bible study and prayer together. Without any obvious clash of personalities our times together were rather a struggle. A number of the group were in demanding jobs during the day. It was hard for all of us to unwind from work and focus on the theme for the evening. So we decided to spend the first ten minutes of our evening in silence together. Each week someone read a verse of a psalm or prayed a prayer and then we were still.

The mood of the evenings quickly changed. The silence relaxed us all, but more importantly, God began to speak to us in different ways. On one occasion a teacher in the group, who was finding her work particularly stressful, described two pictures that had come into her mind as she sat in silence. In the first, she saw an empty crisp bag blowing along a pavement. She immediately identified with what she saw. 'That's how my job makes me feel – empty, blown around and rather worthless,' she said. In the second picture she saw some seaweed on the surface of a very stormy sea; it was being violently tossed about by the waves. The picture then moved beneath the waves, and there she saw that the seaweed was firmly anchored to a rock on the sea bed. Moved and challenged by these pictures, we discussed and prayed together about their meaning and how our lives could be more strongly rooted in God's love and presence.

Another example shows how quietly and undramatically silence can bring a prophetic edge to practical planning and understanding. I spent an evening with the church council trying to plan a ten-day mission in the parish. After some initial talking it was not at all clear what shape the mission itself should take. When I felt that all our own ideas and thoughts were exhausted I stopped the meeting and announced that we would spend ten minutes in silence. During that time I suggested that we simply offered our thoughts and planning to God and asked for his guidance. As not everyone finds it easy to be still with their eyes closed, I placed a lighted candle on the table as a focus. After ten minutes we resumed our discussion and a clear programme fell into place within twenty minutes. During the actual mission eight months later, I was talking with two church members. They reminded me of that meeting and the silence. Both said that although it felt strange at the time they looked back on those ten minutes as the most significant part of their mission planning.

From another small prayer group comes an example of God's word meeting us exactly where we are – touching exactly our hopes and anxieties. The group were reading a psalm together. After reading it through, instead of plunging straight into discussion about it the leader read the psalm again slowly with silence between each verse. Later on, one person wept as he described how the words of the psalm became his own thoughts and prayers and he had a new sense of God's deep love and understanding of him.

Quite simply, silence seems to give space for God to move and speak. We step aside from the centre-stage. In the silence of reverent, humble waiting and longing, he comes to us. Lovingly and firmly he cuts through our confusion and resistance. 'The word of

God is living and active,' says the writer to the Hebrews (4:12). 'Sharper than any double-edged sword, it penetrates even to dividing soul and spirit, joints and marrow, it judges the thoughts and attitudes of the heart.' If we make space, the Spirit will be our guide and we will know the 'leaping word' among us – speaking, guiding and changing our lives.

For reflection

In your imagination consider how you would have felt in Zechariah's situation. It is worth remembering that Zechariah took into solitude a lifetime's discipline of worship, prayer and Scripture reading. The 'leaping word' in our lives is not the product of a lively imagination. It comes to lives that are rooted in God's Word and open to his Spirit.

Consider your own discipline of Bible reading and meditation. Are you growing in your knowledge and understanding of the Scriptures?

Meditation is 'like a cow chewing the cud or a person sucking their favourite sweet'. Next time you read a Bible passage read it through slowly several times. Be silent for a time to let its truth sink in. It may help to have a notebook beside you to make a note of insights or questions to follow up.

Could your fellowship group meeting include some silence together?

Has your church council ever sat in silence over its business together? (If you chair secular business groups, have you considered having a time of silence. Many people work at high levels of stress and the silence could be a great gift to them, as well as pointing to a better way of living and understanding.)

ELEVEN

WITH THE PEOPLE ON YOUR HEART

We do not know what we ought to pray for, but the Spirit himself intercedes for us with groans that words cannot express.

Rom. 8:26

He always lives to intercede . . .

Heb. 7:25

In prayer it is better to have a heart without words, than words without a heart.

John Bunyan

Real prayer is offering what you can see and grasp of what is happening . . . and waiting on God with it, almost as though you have it in your hands.

Alan Amos

Pray! Have I prayed! When I'm worn with all my
 praying!
When I've bored the blessed angels with my bat-
 tery of prayer!
It's the proper thing to say – but it's only saying,
 saying,
And I cannot get to Jesus for the glory of her
 hair.[1]

119

This is such an honest prayer. (Have you ever tried praying when you're head over heels in love?) It reminds us that despite all our best efforts to be 'spiritual', praying remains a gloriously human enterprise. It also illustrates one of our most basic struggles with praying. We have been taught to 'say' our prayers. Our prayers must find words. And even if we know better, it is still hard to let go of the feeling that the only 'real' prayers are those we 'say'. Then our failure to find words feels like the failure of the prayer itself. But of course the deepest prayers of our heart are beyond words. It doesn't mean that prayer is not there. The writer of the poem is so full of prayer that words are just getting in the way. 'It's only saying, saying . . .'

Reduced to silence

On a purely human level there are times when words run out or become clumsy obstacles. Lovers need all the wide spaces of silence to explore the fullness of their love for each other. A friend in grief will need the gift of sensitive presence and touch far more than words. As we have noticed before, silence has a way of expressing presence more profoundly than words. We read that when the friends of Job first came to comfort him, they were so overwhelmed by his suffering that they sat with him for seven days and seven nights without saying a word (Job 2:13). It was perhaps the greatest insight they offered him.

St Paul says that our longings for God are beyond words. They will find expression only in sights or groans. Even creation shares in that groaning – and so does God himself. For, 'We do not know what we ought to pray for, but the Spirit himself intercedes for us with groans that words cannot express' (Rom. 8:26). And by contrast, God reserved some of his strongest rebukes in the Bible for people who said prayers with their lips but not from their hearts (for example, Isa. 29:13). It was one of the signs that they had spiritually lost their way and were living carelessly. Intercession is a costly loving of the world offered out of the depths of our lives. Intercession is praying from the heart not the lips. It takes us deeper than words. In fact, the first sign that we are beginning to pray with real engagement may be that we 'don't know what to say'. Like Job's friends we must first experience the full power and complexity of what we are facing and acknowledge our helplessness. It may be that we are close to real praying when we feel we can't pray.

Before the throne

In the Bible intercession is an activity rather than saying prayers. It involves the whole of us, not just our lips or thoughts. For this reason intercession has been well described as a standing before God with the people on your heart.[2] Now that means we are sharing in what Christ himself is actually doing. We are joining in something that is already happening. In Hebrews, Christ is pictured as the great High Priest who has offered the complete sacrifice for the sins of the world. He has come into the holiest place of God's presence and 'lives to intercede' for the world (Heb. 7:25-7). Using that ancient gesture of prayer, we can imagine him standing, arms stretched

121

out in prayer before the Father's throne. There upon his wounded hands, he offers our world in ceaseless intercession to the Father – 'Father forgive' (Luke 23:34). In fact, if this picture does not express the truth of what is happening, we have no gospel and no hope.

> Look, Father, look on his anointed face,
>   And only look on us as found in him;
> Look not on our misusings of thy grace,
>   Our prayer so languid, and our faith so dim;
> For lo, between our sins and their reward
> We set the passion of thy Son, our Lord.[3]

When we pray for ourselves and our world we are joining in what is going on unceasingly in heaven. Christian prayer is about learning to pray in the praying of Christ. In fact, in a very real sense, there is only Jesus praying. And all the living and longing, the glory and pain of this world, has only one prayer – to be 'found in him' (Phil. 3:9). There, before the Father's throne, we live in the mercy of the world's forgiving and glorious remaking.

The heart of intercession

The question is, what prayer is Jesus praying? If we are to pray with Christ we must find out what is on his heart. Jesus urges us to search hard for it – asking, knocking, seeking and persisting (Matt. 7:7). It means that listening, waiting and stillness lie at the heart of our intercession. We must penetrate beneath the surface of our passing moods, whims and prejudices. We must learn to listen from the heart and so to pray from the heart.

When sharing a house some years ago I found myself increasingly irritated by my lodger. He was actually going through an unsettled time in his own life, but my attitude was unsympathetic. One morning I was praying and routinely 'said' a prayer for him. I sensed a rebuke immediately and fell silent. After a while I saw a picture of a ball of twine that had become hopelessly tangled and knotted. As I watched, I saw one end slowly weaving and unravelling itself from the ball. The meaning was clear to me. I felt God saying firmly to me: 'Look, I know the tangle of this man's life. I know his confusion. And I am unravelling it in my love.' When I prayed again for him my intercession was penitent and from the heart. Some months later I was able to share this with him and when I described the tangled ball of twine he recognised it. It turned out that he was a keen fisherman, and what I described to him was a 'bird's nest' – the hopeless tangle that happens when the line snaps under pressure. The same picture that guided me into deeper prayer, spoke directly to him of God's personal love for him.

There are a few things more painful than kneeling on Church of England hassocks (though sitting on Church of England pews comes a close second I suppose)! Intercession is certainly a discipline, but in many of our churches we have made it painfully hard work. The 'time of intercession' in many services is the low point in the worship. We find it boring and hard to concentrate. We are 'saying' prayers, and it has the feel of a dry duty and discipline. So we need to stop and ask what we are really trying to achieve.

I was once at a meeting to pray for a mission that was happening in another part of the country. I didn't know the churches involved, and although some close friends were on the mission team I found praying almost impossible. I sat there in silence feeling increasingly frustrated. Our attempts at prayer seemed to involve instructing God on what he ought to be doing, telling him about things he already knew about, or telling ourselves how good God was to bolster our deep unease at what we were engaged in. In my sullen and rebellious silence I pictured the cross and the arms of Jesus stretched out as if trying to make contact. He looked to the people on either side of him – the one hard and abusive, the other attentive and longing. Intercession suddenly came alive for me in that moment. Intercession is *not* trying to persuade God to do things he doesn't want to do. It is learning to pray the prayer Christ is praying for the world. And the heart of his prayer is himself – his own life poured out.

To intercede means to 'stand between'. In a divided world the ability to stand between two divided groups and help them to meet and talk again is a priceless gift. At its most homely, it is the gift that enables a host at a party to sit between two strangers and leave them friends. At its most costly, it is the ability to sit with leaders of two countries at war and lead them to trust in each other through their mutual trust in your own mediation. The continued silence on the fate of Terry Waite, the Archbishop's envoy, in Beirut in a constant reminder of the price of such mediation.

Away from the prayer meeting I sat in silence and tried to find a way of responding to that picture of Christ on the cross. I tried again to pray for the town

124

and its mission. I tried to picture the team, with Christ, seeking to inter-cede, to draw people to God. Then I wrote a 'letter' to the people of that town imagining what I would say to them if it was for me to introduce them to God the Father. I then wrote a letter to God the Father, describing what I knew of the town and something of the church's nervousness at having a mission at all. I wrote of their hopes and longings. Then I sat in silence again and found that prayer was alive within me. Words were no longer important. The mission was no longer a remote concern. Though still confused and dimly understood, the intercession had taken flesh in me. I was beginning to pray from the heart. I was moved by the love of Christ for that town and I shared in the anxieties of a people faced with Christ and the mystery of the gospel. With a kind of bitter-sweet pain, I found myself inter-ceding.

Praying at the cross

To intercede for the world with Christ means drawing near to the cross. And the nearer Jesus came to his cross the less he spoke. There is, in the words of one writer, 'an enormous and terrible solitude' around these events. Nor was it unexpected. It was prophesied that the suffering servant of Israel would offer himself in silence. 'He was oppressed and afflicted, yet he did not open his mouth; he was led like a lamb to the slaughter, and as a sheep before her shearers is silent, so he did not open his mouth' (Isa. 53:7). At the trial Mark records how disturbing Pilate found the silence of Jesus (Mark 15:5). Luke tells how Pilate asked him if he was the King of the

Jews. Jesus kept his silence by simply returning the question: 'Those are your words' (Luke 23:3). But his silence was not a helpless, terrified resignation to his fate. It was a willing choice. He had said all there was to say. From now on his intercession was to be his own life poured out.

Christian intercession in the world means drawing near the cross. It will certainly leave us feeling tongue-tied. We must learn the prayer of silence. There is no other way. Reflecting on the awful conflicts in Beirut, a Christian missionary suggested that silence is, at times, the only gift of prayer that is left to offer.

> The difficulty is that words have lost their meaning. For instance, if you mention hope, you might as well be talking about despair for all the effect it has on people. Therefore I would talk mostly of waiting upon God and quietly searching for his presence. Real prayer is offering what you can see and grasp of what is happening, however painful and beastly it is, and waiting on God with it, almost as though you have it in your hands.[4]

This waiting and searching and listening is crucial to Christian prayer. We must be silent to do it. As we have discovered repeatedly throughout this book, silence has a way of awakening and sensitising us to what is around us. A character in one of Chaim Potok's novels tries to explain this to a friend. 'You can listen to silence, Reuven. It has a quality and a dimension all of its own. I feel myself alive in it. It talks to me. And I can hear it.' But he continues, 'You have to want to listen to it. It has a strange and beautiful texture. It doesn't always talk – some-

126

times it cries, and you hear the pain of the world in it. It hurts to listen then. But you have to.'[5]

Praying with the whole of me

How are we to turn such awareness into an offering of prayer? We need alternative ways of expressing our prayer for the world. One of the most helpful rediscoveries in recent years has been the import- ance of the body in prayer and worship. The Bible does not divide up spiritual and physical as if one activity can continue without the other, as we have learned to do. Praying is a physical activity because we are physical flesh and blood. If all our praying is 'in Christ' then it must involve taking flesh, not leav- ing it behind. Praying with Christ will draw us closer to the world around us.

At its most practical this means respecting our bodies when we come to pray. For too long we have neglected them. If our bodies are cramped or bent over or badly balanced on traditional church knee- lers when we pray, we will not be able to concentrate properly. We first of all need a posture in prayer that is relaxed but alert and that allows our breathing to find a natural rhythm (we spoke of this on page 12).

Remember the missionary from Beirut? He spoke of waiting in silence 'offering what you can see and grasp of what is happening, however painful and beastly it is . . . *as though you have it in your hands*'. That simple idea is used quite often for the inter- cessions in services at Lee Abbey. The leader of the prayers invites the congregation to express intercession through three simple movements of the hands:

- hands cupped (as if holding something in them). Here we are invited to give thanks for all that God has given us over the past week. Silence is kept.
- hands reaching out (as if to show God the world around us). We are invited to pray for the world in its suffering and pain (and any particular needs). Silence is kept.
- hands reaching up (as in longing and welcome). We express our hope in the God who comes to the world with healing and salvation. A silence is kept.

Many people found that these simple physical movements focused and deepened their praying. Another suggestion is to use mime or silently to act out prayers. Again, this can be done in a group or alone. There is no right or wrong way to express an idea in movement. You don't have to be an expert. It will be personal to each of us.

Another prayer exercise from Lee Abbey is to bring something to the service that expresses a prayer. It may be a stone or pebble, a leaf or seed, a letter, a newspaper. It can be anything. At a point in the service these items can be brought to the front and placed around the cross on the communion table. There is something very appropriate about praying for our world by the symbolic offering of simple expressions of its life.

In his book *Praying the Kingdom*, Charles Elliott[6] suggests the use of newspapers and imagination to assist our praying for the real world. As we pray for people in the ruins of parts of Beirut or the refugee camps in the Sudan, it may help if we try to visualise their world in our mind's eye. This is a valuable exercise for contemplative prayer groups. It is perilously easy for such groups to grow to love a silence that is of their own making. It is not silence we are contemplating – it is the presence of Christ in the world. We must be willing to have our peace disturbed. To pray in silence with a newspaper headline before our eyes will pull us from the silence of self contemplation into the intercession of Christ.

Praying in the heart of God

Only Christ can teach us to pray for the world. We are seeking what only Christ can give. Our willingness, in the midst of life, to endure and wait and search for the prayer of Christ, is what makes us Christians in this world. We are learning to pray from the heart – not our own, in the end, but the heart of God himself. In the Bible, the heart is the place of our deepest unity of will, understanding, spirit and psyche. It is important to realise this because in our Western culture the heart is seen as the centre of feeling and emotion. What we are looking at here is much deeper than feelings. The heart is the place where our lives are unified and integrated. For this reason the Eastern Orthodox teachers of prayer often speak of putting the mind in the heart. When we live and pray from our moods, impulses and feelings, we are hopelessly fragmented. We need all these fragments drawn into a deeper unity at the heart of our lives. God alone gives this. As we wait in silence before him, the Spirit's work

129

is to bring it all together, and draw it further into the living heart of God's love.

In the end our living, praying, worshipping and interceding are all one. It is we who keep dividing life up into compartments. One of the gifts of silence, quietly punctuating our lives, is to unite and simplify us to live for the 'one thing necessary' (Luke 10:42).

A beautiful story of a monk, on the island of Mount Athos in Greece, draws together the strands of this chapter on prayer. For the writer who introduces him, this particular monk, Staretz Silouan, sums up the meaning and experience of Christian intercession in the world:

> Like all the rest [of the monks] he was quiet and self-effacing. None of his contemporaries particularly noticed him; they were surprised so many people came to see him. Like so many real men of God, he seemed a supremely ordinary person. The workshops of the monastery ran well under his care. Those who asked him anything found that he answered them out of some kind of depth they had not expected. The Russian peasants who came there as migrant workers loved him. And he loved them in a profoundly quiet way. The story goes that he prayed for one, Nicholas, who had left his wife behind and come to earn money.
>
> *'I prayed with tears of compassion for Nicholas, for his young wife, for the little child, but as I was praying the sense of the divine presence began to grow on me and at a certain moment it grew so powerful that I lost sight of Nicholas, his wife, his child, his needs, their village, and I could only be*

aware of God, and I was drawn by the sense of the divine presence deeper and deeper, until, of a sudden, at the heart of this presence, I met divine love holding Nicholas, his wife and his child and now it was with the love of God that I began to pray for them again, but again I was drawn into the deep and in the depths of this again and again I found the divine love for them . . .'

The secret here, and what makes this prayer distinctively Christian, is precisely this alternation. There is joy in the presence of God and yet at the same time a boundless yearning for the healing and fulfilment of all that he has made. The Spirit pushes these men [the monks], these watchers on the edge of life, right into the heart of its central turmoil, and fills their hearts with an agonising yet liberating compassion, a longing for the whole disordered universe to be transfigured by grace. They stand as through with Christ before God before men.[7]

For reflection

A number of suggestions and ideas for prayer are given in this chapter. Alone or in a group explore them as ways of praying for situations in the world.

Why not take actual problems in the world – from the daily newspaper, or real situations known to you or your friends?

TWELVE

HIDDEN TREASURE

His name shall be . . . 'God is with us'

Matt. 1:23

The Kingdom of Heaven is like treasure hidden in a field.

Matt. 13:44

'We always treat our guests as angels – just in case!'
Father Jeremiah, an Egyptian monk

'Surely the Lord is in this place, and I was not aware of it . . . This is none other than the house of God.

Gen. 28.16–17

He is my beginning
he is my end without end
he is for me – eternity.

Isaac of Stella

Exploring silence and solitude can lead us into every corner of life, and to reflect on 'ordinary' life in most practical ways. In fact there is no part of life in which silence and solitude do not have a gift to offer. People often fear that too much silence will dampen everything and make it all rather serious – and

132

indeed I have shown how our feelings about silence reflect our own inner fears. But as you receive the gift of silence, I believe that you will find all of life awakening, deepening and becoming unified in quite unexpected ways. This is a vital discovery to make.

Life in compartments

The Christian message to the world is 'God is with us' – right here in the midst of life. All of life is embraced in the love of Christ. But it is very hard to live as if that is true. It is very hard not to divide up the world into compartments. For example, we instinctively assume we are closer to God in the countryside than in the inner city. It is a very real temptation to be more at home with God in the face of creation than in the face of a man. We look for God in beauty but not in ugliness. But God has chosen to take flesh. And he does not even choose what we consider to be beautiful or special in the world. Quite the reverse: 'He had no beauty or majesty to attract us to him, nothing in his appearance that we should desire him . . . he was despised and we esteemed him not' (Isa. 53:2–3).

The breaking up of our compartments and prejudices can be painful, but it is something that must happen. The late Alexander Schmemann, a great Russian Orthodox theologian, used to tell of a moment of conversion that changed his life in such a way. The story goes that as a young man he was travelling on the Paris metro one day with his fiancée:

They were very much in love and bound up in

133

each other. The train stopped and an elderly and very ugly woman got on. She was dressed in the uniform of the Salvation Army and she came and sat near them. The young lovers began to whisper to each other in Russian, exclaiming to each other about the grossness and ugliness of the old woman. The train came to a stop. The old woman got up and, as she passed the two young people, she said to them in perfect Russian: 'I wasn't always ugly.'[1]

Perhaps we don't have to hurt each other to learn this lesson. Alan Jones writes of a visit he made to a desert monastery in Egypt. A very elderly monk, Father Jeremiah, looked after him. He was a man of indeterminate age and there was a deep gentle silence about him that came from years of solitary prayer, living in caves in the wilderness. Father Jeremiah brought him refreshments and then said, with a deep laugh, 'We always treat our guests as angels – just in case!'[2]

Holy places

God is not closer to us in a church than in a supermarket. He is not more alive in the country than in the inner city. We must constantly refuse the suggestion that he is 'here' but 'not there'. We are simply reflecting our own preferences and prejudices. Of course there are moments when God is more real to us than at others. There will be times and places where God meets us in special ways. But we must beware of a kind of spiritual apartheid that separates our 'holy places' from the rest of life. The surest guard against this is the discipline of silent contemplation. Away from the surface of life, with all its superficial judgements and petty discriminations, we learn to recognise and reverence the deeper source of life in all things.

After I was ordained I worked in a parish in north-west London. I always tried to start the day with some silent prayer, asking to be aware of God's life in the coming day. My Sunday routine meant an early walk to the church down a deserted High Street. It took me under a grimy railway bridge, past a pub and a rather drab row of shops. The pavement was filthy with litter and the remains of takeaways (before and after consumption), from the night before. It was always an uninspiring start to the Lord's day!

But one particular Sunday I turned into the High Street, and knew it was a holy place. It was the same old road, but God was there. I stopped in my tracks and slowly drank in the realisation that all this dirt and drab greyness was soaked in something holy. It was so improbable. In that Presence everything felt infinitely loved – and infinitely lovable. I wanted to laugh and cry and stay silent all at once. I wanted to dance for joy and hide in fear. But perhaps the most abiding sense of that vision was the realisation that this was no 'special' visit. What I glimpsed in that moment was the longing, abiding Presence that held all of life through its mad, headlong flight – the Presence that we would soon drown out again with the roar of traffic and trampling humanity. It was new to me because previously I had neither the eye nor heart to perceive it. 'Surely the Lord is in this place, and I was not aware of it . . . This is none other than the house of God' (Gen. 28:16–17).

Hidden treasure

Jesus always taught that the most important things in life are not found on the surface. Although clues are everywhere, the Kingdom of God is never so revealed as to be obvious. It is like treasure hidden in a field or the pearl hidden, improbably, in the rough hard shell of an oyster. Its power is concealed in the tiniest things – the seed that will one day be the greatest of trees, the small piece of leaven that will swell the whole batch of dough. And the Kingdom of God is revealed to those who are explorers, who knock, and seek and ask and dig beneath the surface until the treasure of life is uncovered. Even the secrets of our lives, says Paul, are 'hidden with Christ in God' (Col. 3:3).

To be alive in this world is to participate in mystery. If the disciplines of silence and solitude remind us of nothing else, it is that we are part of something much bigger than ourselves. All that we see barely touches the greater world of what is unseen. A sense of mystery in life humbles us. It teaches us to treat questions with reverence and handle truth with care. Even the most ordinary things conceal secrets of the Kingdom. Of course Christians are not alone when they seek to live by faith rather than sight. Although our scientific and rational age creates an illusion of control and certainty, we actually live by a much greater measure of faith and trust than we would care to admit. The real question is where, and in what, we place our trust.

Down the centuries Christians have always understood that life is a participation in a holy mystery. In fact the study of the Scriptures was always called 'Mystical Theology'. Mysticism today has become associated with the paranormal and eccentric religious experiences. It has become a fringe interest that the traditional church views with suspicion. In fact all true understanding of God must be mystical. It is mystical because the God revealed in the midst of life is gloriously greater than we will ever grasp or express. Unless it is rooted in the mystery of God's living presence, all our theology and doctrine is sterile second-hand reporting. We think of 'orthodox' Christians as being people who have right beliefs, but the meaning of orthodoxy is really 'right glory' (*doxa* = glory). A Christian is someone who is caught up in the glory of God's love in Christ – someone who lives in a glorious mystery. For how can mortality understand immortality or humanity 'know' divinity? The truth revealed in a man from Nazareth leads us into the unseen glory and mystery of heaven. To *explain* it all is quite beyond us – and so it should be! But Christians are called to be *witnesses*. Christian testimony in the world must always reflect this. We declare our faith in what we do not know as confidently as in what we do know. So it is that St John Chrysostom can write:

Let us invoke him as the inexpressible God, incomprehensible, invisible and unknowable; let us avow that he surpasses all power of human speech, that he eludes the grasp of every mortal intelligence, that the angels cannot penetrate him, nor the seraphim see him in full clarity, nor the cherubim fully understand him, for he is invisible to the principalities and powers, the virtues and all creatures without exception; only the Son and the Holy Spirit know him.[3]

John Chrysostom is not saying we can know nothing about God. But our minds alone will never understand God. We meet him through love. Love teaches us in quite different ways. For example, a first-class degree in the Psychology of Emotion will not help us to 'know' that our husband or wife 'loves' us. That is a different kind of knowing. And unless we are hopelessly arrogant there is always a sense of 'wonder' (mystery) that we should be the object of such love.

So John Crysostom was writing about a faith rooted in the revelation of God in Christ and in the Scriptures. He would be the first to acknowledge that being a Christian will stretch our minds to its limits. But in Christian faith and worship we are constantly drawn beyond what we see and grasp into the glory and mystery of the unknowable.

The silence of eternity

We are not seeking silence. Not even the insights and stillness that silence brings. We are seeking God. God is a friend of silence for 'only silence shares something of God's infinity'. In the midst of our daily lives we seek the eternal source of all life. And Jesus tells us that he seeks us too. Our silence is a humble confession of our mortality, and a celebration of the glory of divine mystery. Our silence, in the midst of life, is the silence of loving and longing for the living God. In him we live and move and have our being.

He himself is my contemplation
he is my delight

138

him for his own sake I seek above me
from him himself I feed within me

he is the field in which I labour
he is the fruit for which I labour

he is my cause
he is my effect
he is my beginning
he is my end without end

he is for me
eternity.[4]

NOTES

Introduction

1. I have borrowed this image from 'Prayer at Night', by Jim Cotter. He is the author of a number of beautiful books of prayers and founder of the 'Cairns Network'. Details from Revd J. Cotter, 47 Firth Park Ave, Sheffield S5 6HF

Chapter 1. Getting Alone

1 This idea is beautifully explained by Catherine de Hueck Doherty in *Poustinia* (Fount 1977).
2 A prayer stool is very easy to make. For an illustration and dimensions see Brother Ramon SSF, *A Hidden Fire* (Marshalls 1985), p. 212.

Chapter 2. With my Whole Self

1 Sr John Oxenham, quoted by Brother Ramon, in *Soul Friends – a Journey with Thomas Merton* (Marshalls 1989), p. 93.

Chapter 3. Meeting our World

1 T. Merton, *Seeds of Contemplation* (Antony Clarke 1962), p. 41.
2 Cited by kind permission. The full story is told in *The Choice* by Sister Kirsty (Hodder and Stoughton 1982), pp. 134–5.
3 H. Nouwen, *Reaching Out* (Fount 1966), p. 31.
4 T. Merton, *Sign of Jonas* (Sheldon Press 1976), pp. 43–4.
5 Ibid., p. 268.

Chapter 4. Return to the Heart

1 Cited in Alan Jones, *Soul Making – the Desert Way of Spirituality* (SCM Press 1985), p. 64.
2 R. Foster, *Celebration of Discipline* (Hodder and Stoughton 1980), p. 1.
3 See Geoffrey Gerard, *Away from It All – a Guide to Retreat Houses* (Lutterworth Press). See also *Vision* (quarterly magazine published by the National Retreat Centre, Liddon House, 24 Audley Street, London W1Y 5DL; contains extensive details of guided retreats of all kinds around the country.
4 Grove Spirituality Booklet, no. 29, 1989.
5 Brother Ramon, *Deeper into God* (Marshalls 1987).
6 Brother Ramon, *A Hidden Fire* (Marshalls 1985), p. 32.
7 For an extended meditation on this theme alone see Brother Ramon SSF, *Life's Changing Seasons* (Marshalls 1987).

Chapter 5. A Preference for the Desert

1 K. Leech, *True God* (Sheldon Press 1985), p. 127.
2 A. Harvey, *A Journey in Ladakh* (Flamingo 1983), p. 15.
3 Cited by K. Leech in *True God*, pp. 154–5.
4 Ibid., p. 155.
5 K. Leech, *Soul Friend* (Sheldon Press 1978), p. 140.
6 H. Nouwen, *The Way of the Heart – Desert Spirituality and Contemporary Ministry* (Darton Longman and Todd 1981), p. 33.
7 Translation in the Alternative Service Book.
8 Quoted in Leech, *True Prayer* (Sheldon Press 1980), p. 175.
9 P. Seddon, *Darkness* (Grove Spirituality Booklet, no. 5, 1984), p. 24.

Chapter 6. The Fearful Void

1 Mark Medhoff, *Children of a Lesser God* (Amber Lane Press 1980), p. 30.
2 A. Kurtz, quoted by Alan Jones in *Soul Making* (SCM Press 1985), p. 61.
3 D. Bonhoeffer, *Letters and Papers from Prison* (SCM Press 1976), p. 371.
4 A prayer from the late night service of Compline.
5 A. Harvey, *A Journey in Ladakh* (Flamingo 1983), p. 15.
6. T. Merton, *Sign of Jonas* (SCM Press 1976), p. 352.

Chapter 7. Stuffed Owls and Waiting Rooms

1 After Leech, *True God* (Sheldon Press 1985), chapter 5.
2 H. Nouwen, *The Genesee Diary* (Image Books 1981), p. 14.

3 R. Foster, *Celebration of Discipline* (Hodder and Stoughton 1980), pp. 78–83.
4 J. Fowles, *The French Lieutenant's Woman* (Triad Granada 1981), pp. 15–6.
5 Cited in K. Leech, *True God*, p. 157.

Chapter 8. Dust and Glory

1 J. Richards, *Wilderness – the Christian Experience*, pamphlet published by Renewal Servicing, P.O. Box 17, Shepperton, Middx TW17 8NU.
2 P. Seddon, *Darkness* (Grove Spirituality Booklet, no. 5 1984).
3 Quoted in Michael Hollings and Etta Gullick, *The One who Listens* (Mayhew-McCrimmon 1971), p. 153.
4 From the poem 'The Hound of Heaven'.
5 Cited in K. Leech, *True God*, p. 187.
6 Verses from F. W. Faber's hymn, 'My God how wonderful thou art'.
7 Cited in Richard Foster, *The Freedom of Simplicity* (Harper and Row 1981), p. 10.

Chapter 9. The Language of the Mad

1 Morris West, *Proteus* (Collins 1979), p. 184.
2 H. Nouwen, *The Genesee Diary* (Image Books 1981), p. 134.
3 Cited by Esther de Waal in *The Celtic Vision* (Darton Longman and Todd 1988), p. 4.
4 Louis Fischer, *The Life of Mahatma Gandhi* (Granada 1982), p. 311.
5 Cited by Simon Tugwell in *Ways of Imperfection* (Darton Longman and Todd 1984), p. 4; though it has to be admitted that no one claims to fully understand this passage.
6 From an essay entitled 'War and the Crisis of Language', reprinted in *On Peace* (Mowbray 1976), p. 40.

Chapter 10. The Leaping Word

1   Archbishop Trench, *Notes on the Miracles*, commenting on Mark 5:19
2   Michael Harper, *Let my People Go* (Hodder 1977), p. 51.

Chapter 11. With the People on your Heart

1   'Temptation' by G. A. Studdert-Kennedy in *Unutterable Beauty* (Mowbray 1970).
2   See Michael Ramsay, *Be Still and Know* (Fount 1982), ch. 7.
3   Verse from William Bright's hymn, 'And now, O Father, mindful of thy love'.
4   Alan Amos interviewed in *Grassroots* magazine (February 1983).
5   Chaim Potok, *The Chosen* (Penguin 1970), p. 259.
6   Charles Elliott, *Praying the Kingdom* (Darton Longman and Todd 1985).
7   From Simon Barrington-Ward, 'Call to Prayer', (*CMS Newsletter*, January 1977).

Chapter 12. Hidden Treasure

1   Cited in Alan Jones, *Soul Making – the Desert Way of Spirituality* (SCM Press 1985), p. 53.
2   Ibid., p. 13.
3   Cited in Thomas Merton, *Contemplative Prayer* (Darton Longman and Todd 1979), p. 100.
4   Isaac of Stella, quoted by Sr Margaret Magdalen, *Jesus, Man of Prayer* (Hodder 1987), p. 73.